Business Research

Business Research
Enjoy creating, developing and writing your business project

Wilson Ng and Elayne Coakes

KoganPage

LONDON PHILADELPHIA NEW DELHI

Publisher's note

Every possible effort has been made to ensure that the information contained in this book is accurate at the time of going to press, and the publishers and authors cannot accept responsibility for any errors or omissions, however caused. No responsibility for loss or damage occasioned to any person acting, or refraining from action, as a result of the material in this publication can be accepted by the editor, the publishers or any of the authors.

First published in Great Britain and the United States in 2014 by Kogan Page Limited

Second Floor, 45 Gee Street	1518 Walnut Street, Suite 1100	4737/23 Ansari Road
London EC1V 3RS	Philadelphia PA 19102	Daryaganj
United Kingdom	USA	New Delhi 110002
www.koganpage.com		India

© Wilson Ng and Elayne Coakes, 2014

The right of Wilson Ng and Elayne Coakes to be identified as the authors of this work has been asserted by them in accordance with the Copyright, Designs and Patents Act 1988.

ISBN   978 0 7494 6895 8
E-ISBN 978 0 7494 6896 5

British Library Cataloguing-in-Publication Data

A CIP record for this book is available from the British Library.

Library of Congress Cataloging-in-Publication Data

Ng, Wilson.
  Business research : enjoy creating, developing, and writing your business project / Wilson Ng, Elayne Coakes.
    p. cm.
    ISBN 978-0-7494-6895-8 (pbk.) – ISBN 978-0-7494-6896-5 (ebook) 1. Business – Research. 2. Business writing. I. Coakes, Elayne, 1950- II. Title.
  HD30.4.N477 2013
  650.072–dc23
                                                                                2013032116

Typeset by Amnet
Print production managed by Jellyfish
Printed and bound in Great Britain by CPI Group (UK) Ltd, Croydon, CR0 4YY

CONTENTS

Introduction

Welcome to your partner for business research!

Your partner recognizes that one of your main reasons for seeking a business degree is to have an opportunity for some research, namely, to make contact with and learn about your favourite business organization or organizations. This is what you mean by research, and you are keen to get started. Maybe you are attracted to the organization's products – stylish consumer items that everyone seems to want, or extraordinary services that compel you to return again and again to use those services – and you are impressed by the leaders of these organizations who have reached out and communicated their vision to you and many others around the world. So you have a desire to learn more deeply about these organizations – the people, products and processes behind their businesses, and to discover why and how they have become successful.

When you began your studies you wanted to know how you could go about this research. Before you started, you already had some knowledge about your favourite organizations or topics, typically from your work experience and market knowledge, but also from your reading, for example, about business strategy and performance. But you also knew that you had to learn a few tools to be able to conduct your research. These tools were your research methods, and in classes and books they were presented as tools that you would use on your journey of research.

Yet you were surprised by what you read and heard in your research methods classes. You were surprised as a student of research methods when you were confronted with complicated jargon that seemed peculiar to the course. You were asked to learn the jargon and make discrete choices from a large number of methodologies and methods.

Although you were prepared to learn, in your mind you were unclear about the point of the choices you had to make.

Accordingly, one of your biggest issues was that you were puzzled as to how the jargon of words in the module could be related to your research. You accepted that research methods were tough to learn (as they are also tough for professional researchers to learn) and you were prepared to invest the time to learn; but having listened to your module lecturers and looked at some of the material, you did not feel any closer to learning about your favourite organization. Teachers and textbooks presented all of the jargon very competently, but you did not see why you should learn an encyclopaedia of methodologies and methods when what you wanted was for someone to tell you clearly and simply the answer to this question: how may I get on and start researching my favourite organization?

This question has motivated us to write this book because we believe we need to clearly connect your use of research methods with satisfying your main aim and interest in getting into your favourite organizations. We recognize your frustration when this aim is not satisfied, and so our aim is for this book to be an indispensable partner at every stage of your business project.

To achieve this aim, we have three objectives:

- First, to provide a clear, step-by-step narrative that will enable you – and the majority of undergraduate and postgraduate business researchers – to get on with your research by making key decisions, and using your chosen research tools simply and effectively.

- Second, to present an easy-to-follow process for you to engage with and to draw relevant and useful research tools for your business project.

- Third, to help you to develop your own view about the issues of interest in your organization in a clearly articulated and interesting story that encapsulates your knowledge about those issues, namely, your prior knowledge of your topic combined with the new knowledge gained from your research.

The way that we link your research methods closely with your findings, and thereby bring together the first and second objectives of this book, is by helping you to develop and present a powerful, persuasive story of your research that will convince examiners of your knowledge. Central to successful storytelling is a well-informed and clearly articulated argument, and this book will help you to develop a strong argument that will form the basis of an interesting and convincing story. The success of this endeavour will then secure you the high project mark that you want.

In seeking to meet these objectives we have omitted a large number of research terms and tools that we believe are ancillary to your core aim of learning about your organization.

Our driving belief behind this book is that research methods, when presented and used imaginatively, can make your journey of research enjoyable. This is the same continuing approach that we take as professional researchers conducting our own research of business organizations. Indeed, we believe that if you are able to learn research methods in a meaningful way, then this is the first step to enjoying your business research, regardless of whether you are conducting a one-off business project. As you will be unlikely to undertake another academic project (unless you choose another course with a project requirement) you should want to make your experience of research as enjoyable as possible and so to do so you will need to learn how to enjoy using the tools of your research, playing with and manipulating your chosen tools – in the same way as you would use any good tool – so that you can meet your learning objectives and realize the fruits of your research.

We believe that if you enjoy your research this will be reflected in your ability to obtain great data. Then, when you develop interesting findings, and draw on your knowledge of the literature to interpret these findings, you will gain a great sense of satisfaction from your ability to understand your favourite organization in a new and profound way. In turn, a logical and clearly articulated process of research will give your examiners every reason to award you a top mark.

Win-win all round.

In student projects, as understanding how to conduct scholarly research is bound with your excitement in researching business organizations, learning about and using research methods can be a personal voyage of discovery, where you learn to select and use techniques in order to locate and focus on one or more areas of business organizations that you are most interested in.

We believe that planning your process of learning and using research methods in terms of a personal voyage of discovering your favourite organizations offers a starting point for enjoying your research. The process of discovering suitable research methods and its outcome in connecting your chosen tools with your research interest will enhance your excitement in learning about your favourite organizations. Here you will feel comfortable with and 'own' the research methods that you choose for your project, where you will shape and apply selected research methods to learn about aspects and areas of your organizations that you want.

So, to get you onto your journey of research – and to enjoy this journey – is the aim of this book. This seems a hard task with lots of choices to make, and then when you've finally made your choices you have no assurance that you will get to enjoy your experience of using your chosen tools. Yet this process of choosing and using your tools, which represents the first part of your journey, can be simple if you can understand how you may enjoy your research without writing off your experience of the journey as a necessary burden. Accordingly, in our vision of every project student enjoying their business research, we want you to start using selected tools and learn – through this book – how to treat them as your personal tools.

How will you do so?

This takes just a little imagination! For example, imagine flying coach class on a long-haul trip. You already know that you can now enjoy flying coach on long-haul if you do a bit of prior internet research and make personal choices in building some flexibility into your schedule, such as in your routing, airlines, seat locations etc. These personal choices go beyond pricing: just as you have no guarantee that paying a higher airfare will produce a more enjoyable trip, so it doesn't follow that enrolling on a more costly student programme will produce a better and more enjoyable experience of research. Instead, your personal choices are about appreciating what specifically to research in your chosen organizations and how to do so.

This analogy of enjoying travelling coach class on a long-haul flight can also be used to develop a deeper understanding of research methods that you may be able to use precisely for your needs. If you spend a bit of time reading about and learning to apply one of the research tools that we suggest in this book, then the chances are that you will enjoy your journey of research much more than if you automatically adopt a research tool – such as the 'case study method' – that you believe to be simple and moreover that many students seem to be using. Learning about and selecting suitable research methods for your project may even earn you a 'freebie' on business class while paying an economy class fare if you can think through and decide on the few choices we present for your research. By doing so you can start immediately on your research.

To capture this value we have brought our experience to bear in suggesting a direct approach to getting started.

While we want to get more students producing high-quality research, our immediate interest is for you to appreciate that enjoying your business research is achievable and important in securing a high mark. This could happen when examiners see your enthusiasm and give you credit for your hard work. Hence, an enjoyable experience of research isn't reserved for 'talented' and 'academically minded' researchers!

What are the right research methods for you and how might you go about selecting them?

First, we will take you through the process of developing a high-quality research project by unpicking some of the academic jargon of research and telling you what it means in plain language. We also suggest which tools of research might be useful for you and how they might help you to enjoy your journey of research.

We then place the most important tools in the context of each part of your research, in a logical sequence where you will use specific tools to help you make decisions so that you can negotiate one part of your research, complete it, and then move on to the next part. To continue with our travel analogy, this is a bit like preparing for a trip abroad where at each stage of your preparation – planning your travel schedule, working out your budget, packing your luggage, deciding on accommodation – you will draw on different tools: maps with which you may plan your journey, and your savings to determine your budget, weather forecasts to tell you what clothing to pack, and local guidebooks to fix value-for-money accommodation. With a modicum of preparation you can make suitable decisions for yourself that will help you to enjoy your destination once you arrive.

We begin by explaining the rationale for and nature of the scholarly research of today's business organizations, before moving on to set out a process of research that meets your profile as a novice small business researcher. In developing the structure of this book, we have followed the same structure as in a typical project report for your business research and present our comments and advice in two parts. In Part 1 we set out certain key choices that you need to make when you wish to get started on your project, while in Part 2 we offer detailed advice on how you may implement each of the key choices in your research, and how different outcomes and results may be derived from using alternative research methods. Part 3 guides you in interpreting and reporting your findings, and Part 4 suggests how you may write a high quality project report based on your findings. In all Parts of this book we present our advice in the form of important, frequently asked questions that you will need to address in preparing for your journey of research:

Part 1: Planning your project

1. The nature of business research. What is scholarly literature, what is the nature of scholarly theory, and how will you select suitable literature and theory and use them effectively for your research?

2. Research methodologies and research methods. What is research methodology, how does research methodology differ from research methods, and why does it matter that you should know the distinction? Importantly, how will you choose and use a suitable methodology and one or – preferably – more research methods for your project?

Part 2: 'Doing' your project

3. Going into the 'field' of your research. First, you need to write up your project proposal from all your planning! This is a requirement of your business project and should also provide you with an outline of your research that you can then develop. We suggest detailed steps for you to prepare a credible, passable project proposal.

Then, having submitted your proposal, you wonder how you may use your chosen tools to collect 'good' data. Specifically, how will you be able to get the data you want? What if you cannot get the data you want? The rest of this part is divided into the chapters that accompany, step-by-step, the procedures you should adopt in developing, implementing and reporting on your project:

4. Collecting quantitative data

5. Collecting qualitative data

6. Collecting ethnographic data

7. Case study research

8. Less common methods of collecting data

9. Ensuring data saturation

Part 3: Reporting your findings

So when you get 'good' data, what exactly do you do with them?

10. Analysing quantitative data

11. Analysing qualitative data

Part 4: Writing your report

12. Discussing your project findings. We suggest how you may report your findings and produce valuable contributions to your chosen literature in a way that satisfies your project requirements and gains you high marks.

13. Conclusion to your report: What are some implications from your quantitative findings for further research in your topic or how will you generalize from your qualitative study to other contexts beyond your specific research?

14. Reference lists

15. And your final task is to write a succinct abstract that captures your topic, your project findings and contributions from your work.

16. The conclusion to your book comprises a set of reflections on the value you should derive from using this guide in your research. We ask: what have you learned and how may your learning make a difference to your business project?

Finally, we suggest a few tips on sorting your references with the aid of software – plus a bit of common sense, all of which will save you time and gain you a few extra marks.

Now, read on, use your book, and start enjoying your business research!

PART ONE
Planning your project

01
The nature of business research

The following two chapters focus on how you may start planning your research. In conceiving and developing your research plan, this chapter presents and explores the first of two key issues that you will need to get a clear understanding of and make a decision on. The issue in this chapter concerns scholarly literature and how you may first select a suitable body of literature and second a suitable theory from your chosen literature to guide you in your research.

Questions you will be able to answer after completing this chapter:

- What is scholarly literature and how will I be able to select and use suitable literature for my project?
- What is the point of a research question (RQ) and how will I be able to develop a single, good RQ that motivates and drives my research?

Key points that you should take away from this chapter are:

- a clear understanding of how to develop a strong, motivating RQ;
- a clear understanding of a number of distinctions between literature on business in the popular press and scholarly literature, and their implications for your research; and
- an ability to select and apply scholarly theory in planning and developing your research project.

What is scholarly literature?

Let us begin your journey of research by helping you conceptualize key aspects of your journey that you should familiarize yourself with and make initial decisions on. Based on these decisions on initial concepts, we will then plan with you a number of concrete steps for your journey. The aim here is to help you prepare, as comprehensively as possible, a plan for your upcoming journey of research before you embark on the operations stage of what researchers call 'fieldwork'.

In an academic project, the place to begin is with literature. This literature concerns specific knowledge of a discipline that you like and are familiar with in business and management studies. We will discuss disciplines later, but first we want to focus on what you should draw from your chosen literature for your business research. In class and in your textbooks you learn that your business research should start with a business problem. That problem, you are told, is derived from your reading of the academic literature in your discipline, and you need to draw on your research to contribute to that literature. These are the 'rules' of research that have been drilled into you. Again, however, you're puzzled by these rules that seem to draw you away from your core interest in your organization. You ask: why do I need a business problem when all I want is to do a bit of research on my organization? Moreover, why do I need academic literature to tell me about business problems? Can I not learn about business problems by reading *The Economist* or the *Financial Times?*

In addressing these questions, let us turn again to our analogy of your holiday. Imagine as a student that you have limited money for a holiday, and yet you want to have a great holiday at the best holiday location. A package holiday is a possible solution – just as in a business project you might pick up a business magazine and choose a packaged or pre-designed project from the internet – see, for example: http://blog.evernote.com/blog/2011/02/11/evernote-for-students-the-ultimate-research-tool-education-series [accessed 13 August 2013].

However, you know that you won't learn a great deal about your favourite organization by picking a pre-designed project from the internet shelf – just as you know that you are unlikely to have an adventurous holiday by booking a package holiday on a cruise ship.

The problem is that pre-designed projects were never designed for you to enjoy your business research but merely to produce a business project that satisfies set requirements, for example, those of a business research module.

By contrast, academic research in business studies is produced by researchers who seek to understand business problems by reviewing previous research in and around the focal topic.

The point of this review is to learn what is already known about the problems that you are interested in exploring. You may be surprised to discover previous studies that have already researched your problem! Even where you believe that no prior studies exist on your particular problem, there will almost always be literature based on research in and around your area of interest that may be applied to your problem. Research that generates scholarly knowledge is capable of being generalizable and applicable to addressing business problems beyond the specific context in which the research was originally conducted. This is due principally to academics' use of theory – or scholarly theory, as academics call it, as the theories are developed from painstaking scholarship – as a basic building block for their research. Academic literature therefore differs fundamentally from business magazines and newspapers in its focus on using and applying theory to guide research and help researchers to make sense of their findings.

In the same way, in your academic business research we want to guide you on the pathway of searching for and using scholarly theory to research and analyse your topic. The academic literature should therefore be *the* source for you to seek out your business problem. It is from this literature that you can build a project where you can make a contribution from your project findings to your chosen literature. If you imagine that the literature on your topic comprises the repository of knowledge on your topic then we hope you will understand what we mean.

As an alternative way of understanding the important role of academic literature in your project, imagine planning your holiday by first reading literature of previous travellers' experiences of your destination. Imagine those travellers as researchers. Further, imagine reading literature that explains and predicts the kind of holiday experience you will have based on your choices of budget, accommodation, objectives etc. Explaining the phenomenon or phenomena of your interest – typically their nature and/or processes – and predicting possible outcomes from your research are what scholarly theory is about. In the same way that your travel literature may offer different explanations and predictions for different holiday experiences based on your input choices, you may also have a number of theories to choose from depending on your research interest.

We believe that it is useful for you to think of theory in this way, as a useful resource for explaining phenomena and predicting outcomes, because good theory is intensely practical. At this point let us introduce our analogy of theory as an accurate weather forecast. We like the analogy of theory as a weather forecast for your project. Just as a good weather forecast explains the conditions of a given locality and predicts likely weather patterns based on a mixture of knowledge from research, the experience of forecasters, and software modelling, so theory that has been developed by scholars from the same bases (save for software modelling which in qualitative theories is usually not applicable) should be used by you in your research as a useful tool a) to explain the phenomena behind your RQ and b) to 'predict' (or humbly suggest, as a student researcher!) the applicability of your research findings beyond the context(s) of your student project. Examiners will expect to find these a) in the Discussion chapter of your project report and b) in your Conclusion. Please see the respective chapters below on writing up your Discussion and Conclusion of your project report.

The main purpose of scholarly theory is to guide you in your process of research. We will suggest more specifically how theory guides you but first let us say that theory is indispensable in an academic project where you are required to make a contribution. As this contribution is firstly to your chosen literature, theory offers a basis for you to make a contribution in your business project by building on ('extending') knowledge of some aspect of your chosen literature. If you successfully extend knowledge then you will have met this key requirement of many business project modules (please check your own university requirements to verify if you are required to make a contribution in your project and, as precisely as possible, what kind of contribution you need to make). Here the role of theory is to lead you through the 'territory' of your research that is unfamiliar to you, for example by offering a reference point for you to compare your findings with what is already known as you try to develop a contribution from your research.

What might this unfamiliar territory be?

Again, imagine going on a holiday to a place you've never visited before. Prior to your trip what tools would you call on to provide you with knowledge of your destination? Consider that you need enough knowledge not just to plan your trip but to choose between different destinations and activities in a location and to guide you to do precisely what you want to do. Precision is important to you because you have a budget and limited time and you need to know in advance what it will cost and what you will get for your investment.

Theory can fill this role, and the advance knowledge that theory in your chosen literature can offer is not just information.

You want one or more tools to explain key attractions in a location:

- What each of those attractions is.
- Why any of the attractions should interest to you.
- To predict what you have to do (for example, cost, accommodation, transport) to get the enjoyment you will come to expect having understood and chosen the destination you want.

Good theory provides a useful tool to explain a phenomenon of your interest and to predict what you are likely to get from your research – namely, your anticipated outcomes from this research before you embark on your journey. This is true whether your investigation takes the form of your visit to an attraction in a far-away location or whether it concerns your research into a puzzling question about your favourite organization.

At this point may we sound a note of warning based on a typical *faux pas* by project students: Scholarly knowledge that is generated from your academic research must *not* be confused with market research.

Market research is generated by professional consultants who are hired by clients and who seek only to satisfy their requirements. The focus of consulting reports is therefore on producing results and recommendations that suit their paying clients. In this scenario market consultants are seldom interested in scholarly theory, there is little contribution to literature, and the findings of previous research are often immaterial to their work.

How do I develop a good research question (RQ)?

If you believe – as we do – that fun and adventure go together, then the better you plan your adventure the more you are likely to enjoy your experience of it. In our scheme of things it doesn't matter where you decide to go, just as there are no subjects or topics of research that are more or less likely to score high marks. Better planning in your research starts with a clear and do-able RQ: 1) that you can fully answer within the brief few months of your student project; and 2) that captures your interest in your organization and therefore continues to motivate you in your research.

A single, powerful RQ is your first requirement in your business project as it provides a key rationale for your research. Specifically, a good RQ keeps you motivated to see your research through to completion. A good RQ will also captivate your audience of examiners and readers by signalling to them the importance, relevance and possible contribution of your project. It follows therefore that you will have given yourself a great opportunity to score a top mark by developing a good RQ and by then proceeding very clearly to answer your RQ in a full, convincing and imaginative way. (See Table 1.1 for a few examples of RQs from past student projects and Table 1.2 for examples of words and concepts drawn from various areas of business and management studies for you to use to develop a topic for your research.)

Your RQ then becomes the main yardstick by which your project will be judged. You want this to happen as a good RQ should work in your favour. This thinking is no different from the way you would normally plan a memorable and enjoyable holiday adventure by spending a lot of time planning, developing and refining what you want to see and do in the limited time and budget that you have.

So, start thinking about your project by first thinking through a single, good RQ that motivates you in your research. Typically, what motivates you will be what you wish to find out about your organization. Initially, this might be as fuzzy as the 'secrets' of its success. If so,

TABLE 1.1 Examples of motivating and researchable RQs from past student projects

Marketing	
When and why are customers disloyal?	How do new businesses develop strong brands?
	Why do established businesses need strong brands?

Business strategy	
1. What is a business model?	How do high-technology start-ups develop business strategy?
2. Why do companies need business models?	

Human resource management ('HRM')	
1. How may talent be managed in a creative business?	1. Why do ambitious professional managers work for family businesses?
2. What is the nature of leadership in a creative business?	2. Is conflict in family businesses (or another type of organization) a bad thing?

Finance	
1. What is the relationship between 'good' corporate governance and performance?	How efficient are small/big businesses?
2. How may owners of small businesses be monitored and controlled?	

TABLE 1.2 Some popular words/concepts in business and management studies (listed alphabetically)

Marketing

Branding	Customer value, Value proposition	Demographic segmentation, behavioural segmentation	Relationship marketing	Distribution channels

Business strategy

'Competitive advantage' (Porter, 1980)	(Long-term) vision	Innovation management	Resources and capabilities	Success factors

HRM

Benchmarking	Employee relations, compensation and rewards	(Workplace) ethics	Human capital management	Performance management

Finance

Finance terms, eg equity–debt, credit–debit, assets–liabilities, benefits–costs	Performance (outcomes)	(Financial) incentives	Monitor and control (behaviour, systems)	Residual costs and claims

you will develop this interest as you read the academic literature that you plan to use for your project, and you will frame your interest in terms of the language in your chosen literature. Framing your interest in this way will give you a sound basis for a motivating and researchable RQ. Motivation is a core purpose of your RQ as your enjoyment of your research will depend on how far your RQ captures what you want to research and therefore on the extent to which your RQ motivates you to do the research that you want.

The following are examples of motivating and researchable RQs from past student projects. These examples are meant only for you to understand what good RQs have previously been developed and for you to get a sense of why they were motivating and researchable RQs. The list is not intended for you to copy, and you are encouraged instead to experiment with and develop a researchable RQ – based on the criterion of your chosen literature, as suggested in the previous paragraph – that will personally motivate you. The common, relevant point in these RQs is that they were all interesting as they raised a puzzling problem which was of personal interest to the respective researchers based on their knowledge of key issues in their chosen literature. Further, the RQs were researchable in the organization(s) that the researchers were interested in and within the six- to eight-month time frame that is normally available, in practice, to student projects.

How may I use scholarly literature in my project?

Your thoughts on your RQ will be based on your knowledge of the body of literature behind your project.

This section explains the nature and purpose of scholarly literature and why and how students' choices of literature form the foundation of their project. The process of choosing suitable literature is articulated, in which a single, good RQ that captures your research interest emerges from your chosen literature. We then proceed to suggest how your RQ may be developed, and how this RQ then drives your subsequent research and your write-up of an interesting story of your topic based on your research.

First, where will you find academic literature?

Academic literature – or scholarly literature as academic research-ers call their published work – comprises a body of knowledge in one of a number of constructed disciplines, many of which are used by both corporate executives and business academics who work in departments that 'specialize' in functions within each discipline and who use their specialized knowledge in the work that they do. Prin-cipal examples of these disciplines that typically form the backbone of companies and business schools are marketing, business or corpo-rate strategy (often marketing and business strategy departments are combined as the expertise in both areas is seen to be closely related), accounting and finance, human resource management (HRM), infor-mation and knowledge management, and operations management.

Academic researchers have drawn on these very porous divisions and considerably expanded them by creating new areas of knowledge and expertise. Many of these areas, such as international business and organization studies, embrace and 'cross over' a number of con-ventional business departments and academic disciplines. Academic researchers refer to all of these areas of knowledge and expertise as 'topics'. This meaning of 'topic' is very different from the conception of many students who typically conceive of 'topics' only in terms of their chosen subject or case company for their research, such as supermarkets in the United Kingdom (subject) or AN Other (case) firm selling branded goods in Thailand.

A research topic means much more than a subject or case company and refers primarily to the academic discipline (eg marketing, HRM etc) from which you will draw your knowledge and expertise for your own research.

Therefore, at the outset of your project, choose an academic dis-cipline where you may locate your research so that you can then draw knowledge and expertise from published scholarly research of your chosen topic. This foundation will give you resources for you to then start building and developing your project. While doing so, you will follow a clear and well-trodden path that your supervisors and examiners can easily follow, and of course the easier it is for them to follow your research and your report, the more assured you will be of scoring a high mark for your project.

How may I use theory?

We have explained the nature and purpose of scholarly theory on pages 12–16 above. Moving on from our discussion, we want to suggest how you should draw on scholarly theory:

1. to develop knowledge that extends existing work without 'reinventing the wheel' and merely repeating what other researchers have already found; and

2. to be guided by the theoretical and methodological frameworks that prior researchers in and around your chosen topic have used for their own research.

Fulfilling both 1 and 2 requires you to offer a contribution to your chosen literature for your project, and of course any contribution is predicated on your prior knowledge of the literature. You must be familiar with the core pieces of literature in and around your topic, and there is no substitute for this knowledge in preparing for your research.

Drawing on our travel analogy, would you really want to risk travelling to an unfamiliar environment without first reading up on it? Of course, you might be a risk taker or thrill seeker! Academic research on the other hand is about building knowledge, principally knowledge of your chosen literature, by learning about the organizations of your interest. Research therefore is not simply about researching. The former will gain you high marks but not the latter. Accordingly, it makes sense to get as clear as possible an idea of what has been researched and found before seeking to extend knowledge of your topic.

What has been researched and found forms the basis for good, scholarly theory that is the output for the literature on your topic. Using theory in your research can form a very powerful basis for you to plan and implement your project by guiding you to conduct your research in important areas where there may be a paucity of knowledge. In this way theory can be indispensable in guiding you to extend existing knowledge of a phenomenon by signalling gaps in the literature on your phenomenon. Recall, for example, how Porter's theory of competitive advantage (1980, as described below) has spawned research of this phenomenon across a vast spectrum of institutions and organizations around the world.

Further, theory can also motivate and drive your research in an effective way that addresses your RQ. As theoretically driven research is a sound, proven way to produce meaningful findings from your research, you will be able to maximize your enjoyment of this research with satisfaction that you are progressing in the right direction down a well-trodden path.

The problem, however, with theory is that many students (and corporate managers) have a preconceived view that theory is merely a tool for academics and not for 'real-world' people. This view may have been influenced by academics with little experience of academic research who see a gulf in perspectives on higher education between research and researchers on one side, and teaching and teachers on the other.

In business research, perhaps the only relevant aspect of this old debate between business researchers and teachers is that theory in fact forms an essential link between these two roles and entangles them inseparably.

This is because theory is a body of knowledge derived from scholarship that provides a framework for both researchers and teachers to develop and disseminate knowledge to everyone in their chosen areas. In this conception, theoretical knowledge that can guide your research and offer informed knowledge would offer a sound and well-proven pathway in developing your contribution from your research.

'How then may I choose suitable theory for my project?' The answer to this question can be very simple. Although you may choose any theory for your topic, actually the literature in your topic area contains theories specific to that area. Choosing suitable literature for your research will therefore provide you with a number of 'ready-made' theoretical perspectives that may, often with just a little imagination, be applied to and guide your research.

So, start choosing a suitable theory by selecting academic literature for your project that you are most familiar and comfortable with.

To do so, review the reasons that prompted you to research your favourite organization in the first place. What were you interested in learning? For example, if you were to articulate your interest in your organization's 'secrets of success' in terms of strategic factors, then this interest might place your research in the business strategy literature. Here existing theories of competitive advantage may guide your research by suggesting where you might look for success factors and what those factors might be.

In this example consider Michael Porter's theory of business competitive advantage (1980), an 'old' (in business strategy terms) theory popular with students and teachers which has been revisited recently (Porter, 2008).

This theory suggests that competitive advantage occurs when an organization acquires or develops an attribute or combination of attributes that allows it to outperform its competitors. Now, say you were interested in researching the competitiveness of your chosen organization and the extent to which it may develop a competitive advantage over its rivals. Here you might choose to adopt Porter's theory of competitive advantage to guide your research of this topic. If so, you may then read Porter's 'guidebook' on competitive strategy (1980) and apply his 'Five Forces' framework to guide your research of this phenomenon by first exploring what resources and capabilities your organization might possess, and second, by meticulously examining the extent to which any of the resources you have located have the ability to generate competitive advantage.

As in this example, your choice of theory is driven by: a) the literature written by research scholars such as Michael Porter that best captures your interest in the organization of your research; and b) keywords that relate your interest with the particular 'language' of literature that draws on those keywords.

Here, for example, keywords such as 'success factors' can relate to the language of business strategy, although not exclusively so as many keywords may be shared among one or more disciplines. So, success factors may also be viewed in terms of criteria for financial performance in the finance literature and in terms of marketing strategies.

Our point is that while keywords offer you a starting point for locating your literature you will need to know the literature in your chosen disciplines pretty well and then consider how far you are personally comfortable with using that literature to guide your research. By contrast, students sometimes read up on their literature after their research, which of course would then produce highly questionable contributions. All this may be avoided if you tailor your project around the literature that you are most familiar and comfortable with, and not the other way around, given a typical need to contribute to your chosen literature.

Table 1.2 provides a list of keywords used in literature in different business and management disciplines. Please note that our list is intended merely to suggest a number of distinctive words and concepts that are associated with and used by writers in each subject, and the list is not by any means exhaustive.

References

Porter, M (1980) *Competitive Strategy: Techniques for Analysing Industries and Competitors*, Free Press, New York

Porter, M (1990) *The Competitive Advantage of Nations*, MacMillan, Basingstoke

Porter, M (2008) The five competitive forces that shape strategy, *Harvard Business Review*, 86(1), pp 78–93

02
Methodology and methods

Now that you have gained a good grasp of the purpose of scholarly literature in your research and how you may use theory to develop it, we now present and explore the second of two key issues that you will need to get a clear understanding of and make a decision on before embarking on your research. The issue in this chapter concerns your research methodology and research methods and how you may select a suitable methodology and a number of methods to 'operationalize' your research – meaning, to enable it to 'go live' as a viable project.

Questions you will be able to answer after completing this chapter:

- What are the key research methodologies and research methods that I should learn, and why do I need to understand differences between methodology and methods?

- How do I select a suitable methodology and methods for my project?

Key points that you should take away from this chapter are:

- a clear understanding of the main distinctions between research methodologies and research methods and of a small but important range of methodologies and methods;

- a strong grasp of which research methodology may be most suitable for you given your ontology, epistemology, and your research interests;

- a clear understanding of the bases upon which you may choose popular research methods, namely surveys and interviews; and

- a strong grasp of how you may develop the key skill of listening in order to become a good academic interviewer.

What is research methodology?

Many textbooks on research methods suggest that methodology is about your 'research stance'. By research stance, researchers mean your core beliefs about the nature of things in the world ('how things are in the world') that lie behind the key choices in your research.

A range of possible research stances is presented, and you are asked to choose a suitable stance that matches your beliefs about what constitutes 'facts' in the world (ontology) and about how and what you choose to define as 'facts' (epistemology). It is then suggested that your ontological and epistemological stance will inform your project's research design (your design or framework comprising the approach you propose to take and tools you will use for conducting your research).

1) Ontology – or different conceptions of a dream holiday

While you appreciate that building your research design requires you to make a number of decisions, you – and many other research students – are puzzled by the complicated, jargon-heavy way in which research is presented, a presentation that pricks the enjoyment of doing research.

A key problem of research in student business projects seems to be that learning about a range of ontologies and epistemologies does not explain how you may get started with your research.

Specifically, in conceptualizing (namely, considering alternative choices about and deciding on your approach to) your research project you need to know:

- the distinction between research methodology and research methods;

- why business researchers need to decide on their research methodology; and

- how they may do so (and clearly state their chosen research stance in their project reports).

Let us look at the second question first and leave the first question to the next subsection (What has methodology got to do with research methods, page 41).

To do so, let us again turn to our holiday analogy at the stage where you are considering alternative choices (type of holiday, destination, budget) for your holiday. In this example, let us elevate the importance of the holiday you are looking for by inviting you to imagine a 'dream holiday'.

Suppose that there are two different individuals planning two very different types of a 'dream holiday'.

First, imagine for a moment that you are a wealthy (and trendy) shareholder of your family business with a vast sum of cash at your disposal. In this scenario you are not constrained by any budget, and as a trendy person you have a view of a dream holiday that is about indulging in a luxurious experience on a faraway beach where everything is done for you and you do nothing for your entire holiday. You think 'this is paradise,' and surely everyone will have the same and will want the same experience. So this must be the only possible view of a dream holiday.

Consider, however, an alternative scenario of a dream holiday.

Imagine that someone else believes that a dream holiday is about being able to use her holiday time as an extended period of paid leave to spend in public service. Imagine that this service could take the form of part-time work, say as a Territorial Army (TA) soldier or as a volunteer with the Red Cross or with Médecins sans Frontières. As a TA soldier or a health volunteer you could be sent to a war zone. Now these types of volunteer roles are very real choices for holiday jobs as many volunteer organizations continue to thrive using volunteers on holiday from their full-time jobs. Some even choose to cycle across China to raise money and pay for this experience (http://www.truevolunteer.org/getinvolved/fundraise/, accessed 13 August 2013)!

'Weird', you might think, that anyone would want to spend their holiday doing more work – and risk their life, to boot. But consider if this view of a holiday-as-work really is so weird once you understand that behind the notion of a dream holiday there are many views of the nature of 'work'.

While everyone may want a dream holiday and seek to derive the greatest satisfaction from this rare event, different views of what constitutes work govern conceptions of a dream holiday and may produce different interpretations of the kind of activities that make up a dream holiday. Here, for example, our TA soldier might believe that all holidays should be spent in performing useful and rewarding work, and that 'dream holidays' involve international postings to war zones where the soldier's utility and reward may be highest. By contrast, your view of a dream holiday is just about indulging yourself.

The two views of the nature of dream holidays are therefore quite different and are based on dissimilar beliefs about holidays being a time for indulging yourself (your view) against a notion of holidays as a time for indulging others when the TA soldier is prepared to risk her life to achieve her goal of serving society. Yet both you and the TA soldier believe in and avidly seek your respective 'dream holiday'.

Do you believe that the TA soldier's view of a dream holiday is ridiculous? If so, maybe your view of a holiday is closer to her view than you think. Read on and see why…

Just as people have different views of what constitutes a dream holiday, there are a number of different views that researchers may hold of the world in which they conduct their research.

The view a researcher has of the nature of people and their activities, and of social organizations and culture in which activities are organized and enacted, governs the way that the research is designed, and its findings are analysed and reported.

That view is the researcher's research stance that textbooks talk about and needs to be thought through and an appropriate stance to be adopted that best suits you as a researcher and fits your research.

Let us make this choice practical for you.

In our example of a dream holiday we selected two contrasting views of this phenomenon. Similarly, up to the level of MBA/MA/MSc business research, we believe that you need to really learn just two principal research stances among many research stances. We would be surprised if you have not heard of the two perspectives below, but in your business project you need to reflect on any preconceptions you might have about each of these perspectives, and choose the perspective that really suits your beliefs of the nature of the world.

Scholars call an individual's view of the nature of the world her ontology, and in researching business organizations all researchers need to first decide on their social ontological position – that is, the researcher's personal view of society and organizations – and its related philosophical process, epistemology (see page 33).

Among a number of reasons for this, perhaps the main reason is that you are undertaking a piece of research for yourself and not for anyone else, and you need to first set out your beliefs (in your report) so that your audience of examiners can understand how you have approached your research. This need to communicate your beliefs to your audience is very much like the way that successful scientists (think of Sir Richard Attenborough or Professor Stephen Hawking) and artists (think of Stephen Spielberg or another favourite film director) whose popularity is built on their ability to communicate their views of the world – their social ontologies – through their documentary programme, lecture or movie in a clear, concise and attractive way to a global audience.

The first of two popular social ontologies is objectivism.

Many students (and professional managers) think that they are, or should be, 'objectivists' if they are to conduct a 'professional' piece of research. Objectivism is the belief that most if not all objects we see around us have a given existence that cannot be significantly influenced by social activity, actors or any form of human intervention.

In organizations, an objectivist view holds that social phenomena, including the nature of organizations and organizational processes and culture, have a given existence that employees and all other organizational actors have at best a very limited influence in shaping ('that's the way of the world').

In this view of the way the world, seeking to be as 'objective' as possible is considered a good and desirable aim of social activities as it removes 'subjective' variances in processes arising from human intervention that occlude their 'true' nature.

For objectivist researchers, it follows that an 'objective' research design and report should constitute a 'dream' standard that should always gain a higher mark than a 'subjectively' written report that prioritizes the researcher's views. In other words, objectivists believe that an objective view of the world is superior to a subjective perspective (see Thomas Kuhn's landmark theory (1962) of the way that 'revolutions' in scientific thought have occurred historically following 'paradigm shifts' in popular conceptions of scientific 'truth'). Do you (not) share this view?

Strangely, while you might think that you are – or should be – a social objectivist, you might in fact believe in its opposite, social constructionism or constructivism (same meaning for both words, and we will henceforth call this phenomenon 'constructivism').

Constructivists believe, to a greater or lesser extent, that society is constructed, that *everything* you and others see and experience in every society in the world is constructed, either mostly or completely, depending on the extent of an individual researcher's beliefs in 'constructed' social reality, by individuals and groups of people. As organizations are an integral part of society, and as business and management studies concern the behaviour and performance of people in organizations, the question of your ontological beliefs about the nature of society form a crucial starting point in your research of social organizations and their people.

Constructivists believe that one of the most common and important ways in which the social world constructs 'reality' is through the use of language in conversation (see, for example, how some constructivists view and conduct interviews as ordinary conservations, in Holstein & Gubrium, 1995).

Consider, for example, some of the types of categories and conceptions that people use to define themselves and social artefacts in organizations, typically in oppositional terms: executives and non-executive administrators (people) and standard/high-quality and non-standard/low-quality corporate policies and practices (which are examples of social artefacts).

What, if anything, do you believe exists in society that is not influenced, modified, constructed and reconstructed by humans?

Do you really believe there is such a thing as 'objective' reality?

Or do you believe, to a greater or lesser extent, that what you see in society is a perception, an interpretation of people and social artefacts by other people, and by yourself.

Many students assume, perhaps without questioning themselves, that they are objectivists.

It turns out that many of you think in a constructivist way when you discover that you want to learn how your favourite organization constructs, for example, the nature of your organization's corporate culture and practices, in which its products and services are developed (we are thinking again of your interest in your firm's success factors). By contrast, if you were objectivist you would be interested, for example, in developing 'one-size-fits-all' regulations and policies for all organizations to follow, regardless of any differences in organizational culture. This is because in an objectivist world social phenomena are reducible (either more reducible or less reducible, depending on how far the researcher is objectivist) to a set of commonly shared criteria. Is this what you really want to research? Some students and some researchers do, but in our experience most students do not.

Why some students who believe in constructivism fail to recognize and draw on their beliefs has a number of explanations.

We suggest that one reason why many constructionists adopt, often without question, an objectivist view of the world is rooted in a pro-science bias in education systems around the world that in fact is founded on a false perspective of the 'objectivist' nature of physical and natural science.

This isn't a question of ignorance. Apart from the highly positive impact of the natural and physical sciences in changing human society (which in fact questions how far the natural and physical sciences can be viewed in objectivist terms), an element also exists of institutional and personal power in explaining the dominance of an 'objectivist' view of the world that is arguably stronger and more apparent in totalitarian regimes than in democratic societies. Objectivism has also become a convenient way to constrain the 'subjective' opinions, behaviour, and activities of 'dangerous' individuals whose chief danger lies in their ability to communicate their informed story of social reality clearly and attractively; and in so doing to persuade others to change the societies in which they live.

In sum, objectivists seek to examine, test and produce standardized regulations and policies across social boundaries that minimize variances arising from non-standard, subjective intervention by individuals.

The belief here is that the extent to which individual human variances can be minimized will increase the performance of organizations. This is because the performance of organizations is thought to be an absolute standard with established criteria for its measurement; and the degree to which these criteria are met would then determine the organization's performance. In this objectivist ontology of social 'reality', all social actors are hired to perform standard tasks set out in their contract in as mechanical a way as possible, with rewards and punishments being handed down, respectively, for the extent to which employees conform or fail to conform to set standards.

From an objectivist perspective, you as a researcher might be interested to research the causes of differences between corporate policies and practices, typically in a large sample (as a small sample might prove to be an exceptional and therefore 'unrepresentative' example of your research). Your aim here might then be to align the practices of firms in your field of interest with established industry policies in order to improve corporate performance.

In contrast, constructivism concerns a set of beliefs about the ways in which most, if not all, phenomena in the world may be formed and continuously shaped by social activity and human intervention.

Social constructivists believe that social 'reality' is constructed (that is, controllable and hence changeable) by the activities of social actors. By extension, social construction in working organizations involves a constant process of interpretation and reinterpretation, for example, of an organization's culture as the organization seeks to compete by drawing on its market reputation to win over more customers, and by the attractiveness of internal HRM practices that reward effort instead of merely focusing on success and failure. At the heart of these shaping and reshaping processes in organizations lies the social actor (a term we use generically here although an organization may have many types of social actors with different duties and responsibilities) who may be either an internal or external stakeholder of the organization.

It follows that researchers who are social constructivists believe that a key aim of their research is to present a clear, informed and fundamentally personal view of the social phenomena they are researching. In social constructivist research, as interest is often in the nature and processes of social phenomena, a well-crafted story will score high marks. Let us here consider in a little more detail what we mean by a well-crafted story. Recall our suggestion in Chapter 2 that a strong, well-informed argument based on knowledge of your chosen literature forms the foundation of a good story. Now, if we develop this view by suggesting that your findings form the substance of your story, then a thoughtful interpretation of significant meaning(s) that you have drawn from your story can be a key factor in capturing the interest of your audience of examiners and convincing them of the quality of your research.

Accordingly, a successful research project in a social constructivist exercise would be in the extent to which the work provides a cogent, coherent and fundamentally convincing interpretation of the subjective 'reality' of the phenomenon being researched, typically by the social researcher's ability to draw on her knowledge of her chosen literature and by her fluent and knowledgeable application of research methods to provide a persuasive interpretation of that reality.

In a wholly constructivist perspective, the more intensely personal the subjective input of the researcher, the more chance there is of a powerful and convincing 'reality' of the multiple meanings that might emerge from a socially constructed piece of research.

2) Epistemology – or how do I know that what I believe to be 'facts' about my holiday are actually facts?

In your conception of a dream holiday, have you considered where you got your idea that holidays are about doing nothing? How do you know that your view of a dream holiday is a 'normal' view that is widely shared by co-workers, employees and students? You might think you do not care if people share your view of a dream holiday; but what if in your work it was a part of your employment contract to report on your holiday activities to share with your co-workers and employees? If so, might it be you who are 'weird' for thinking that holidays are about lying on the beach doing nothing?

So, once you have decided what your view of the world is, then you should consider where you got your information from to form and support your view.

What is the basis of your knowledge about society, organizations, culture etc?

Again, let us simplify this decision for you by suggesting just two main sources for your world view, which is known as your epistemology. Recognizing your epistemology – which is shorthand for 'where you got your facts from' – before you embark on your research will guide how you collect and analyse your data and, most importantly for your project mark, how you will interpret your findings. Two possible sources of your knowledge are either positivism or interpretivism.

Please remember that these are not the only sources of knowledge and numerous open websites and research methods textbooks offer you a number of other epistemologies (see for example http://plato. stanford.edu/entries/epistemology, accessed 13 August 2013). However, in keeping with our promise in the Introduction to present an easy-to-follow process for you to engage with and use as a research tool, from our experience we believe that positivism and interpretivism are epistemologies that research students will typically use. Often these epistemologies are used by students and others without clear understanding of how they have been used, and if so our interest is to help you choose between the two epistemologies and to then try and develop and refine your use of either epistemology in the most effective way.

First you need to be clear which ontology relates with which epistemology.

Mixing them up by pursuing a 'mixed methodology' is inadvisable, although using mixed research methods is to be encouraged, as we explain on pages 41–43 below.

Let us start with the historically more prevalent ontology (objectivism) and epistemology (positivism). Objectivism and positivism are natural bedfellows. Where objectivists believe that human agents – individually or in groups – have very limited influence in shaping organizations, the basis of this belief in positivism suggests that research should be about developing and testing hypotheses, and that researchers may collect facts and figures from organizations that exist as concrete entities – in other words, entities that have some verifiable measure of 'truth' about their existence.

The 'scientific' and 'rigorous' way that facts are collected then provides a 'valid' (well-founded and accurate) basis for testing your hypotheses, where the point of testing is not only to accept or reject your hypotheses (and the theory or theories on which your hypotheses are based), but in so doing to test the validity of your 'sampling' – which is your chosen approach in collecting your sample of data.

In the next step, having tested your hypotheses, positivist researchers would then deduce results, and the subsequent findings would be extrapolated beyond their particular contexts to explain the phenomenon under research in other contexts, which can include other organizations, industries and environments. In every event, the results of this deductive research have to be able to be replicated by any other researcher following the same research procedure.

As the attainment of scientific 'truth' is the main objective of positivism, only through a methodology where you deduce outcomes from testing factual data can the 'truth' be established of your phenomena of interest.

Accordingly, students adopting this approach would be embracing a perspective of natural science in their business research and would be conducting their research in the manner of a laboratory test, with the same strict discipline in collecting and analysing data. In doing so students should also note the specific language of objectivism and its knowledge basis in positivism. At all times this language – for example, deducing, testing, assessing, validity, representativeness and extrapolation – should be confined to use within its domains of positivism and objectivism.

Unless students wish to risk being marked down, the language of positivism–objectivism as outlined above should be avoided where students choose to adopt the opposing perspective of constructivism.

The epistemological basis of constructivism is interpretivism.

In business research, an interpretivist epistemology requires the researcher to immerse herself in every part of her project as a core element of its research design.

By 'immerse' we mean that the researcher's personal views of elements of her project – for example, her choice of literature, data collection and analysis – take centre stage in some or all parts of her project. Instead of studiously omitting the researcher (herself) from her research, as an interpretivist, the researcher has a critical role in interpreting and presenting her data to examiners in her own way, being well-informed and telling an original, interesting story.

Therefore, the extent to which the researcher can present a convincing interpretation (explanation) of her chosen phenomenon will gain her a top mark. Now of course researchers may choose the extent of their interpretivism and there is no given rule whether you prioritize your personal perspective in interpreting some or all parts of your project; but whatever your degree of interpretivism, it is imperative for you to clearly state your research stance at the outset of your research methods chapter of your report and explain your rationale for adopting your specific approach to research. Please check the extent to which your university regulations allow you to use an interpretivist approach in your reporting, but equally you should be very careful in distinguishing university regulations from any personal prejudices of supervisors and teachers against contructivism and interpretivism.

Please also note that personal interpretation of a phenomenon based on knowledge is quite different from merely expressing a bald and uninformed opinion!

You need to appreciate if you choose to conduct and present interpretivist research that a convincing explanation of your phenomenon arises from deep knowledge of your chosen literature. Here your ability to persuade examiners to believe your explanation of your phenomenon is based on your skill in moving back and forth from your data to your understanding of your literature in suggesting how and why your data relate (or not) to the literature.

This approach to interpreting your findings by seeking to closely relate your data with your literature constitutes what is known as an 'inductive' process where interpretivists make inferences from their knowledge of their research data and literature in presenting a convincing interpretation of their phenomenon (see, for example, Denzin & Lincoln, 2003 for a detailed explanation of an inductive research process). An inductive approach to research is therefore the opposite of the deductive procedure discussed above, and the two approaches cannot be combined. In interpretivist research, as the gap between researchers' interpretation of the data and their chosen literature is often wider than in objectivist research, presenting a convincing story can be difficult, especially for novice researchers.

Here there is no substitute for deep knowledge of your chosen literature. Further, you should study how to interpret text and analyse what it means in later chapters of this book.

In sum, instead of rejecting subjectivity the interpretivist researcher needs to learn how to embrace her subjectivity by seeking to make sense of the phenomena under research.

Conducting your research by surfacing and presenting your 'I' in the research and write-up is not only encouraged but a necessary element in a communicative and convincing piece of interpretivist research. As interpretivist research, typically based on organization cases of students' chosen phenomenon (see below), is often the most popular choice of research design among our project students, researching and writing convincingly in the first person singular may therefore constitute a vital element in the success of your project.

Assuming you have chosen a case design – namely, a research design that is centred on writing up an account of a phenomenon of your interest, for example, your organization's competitive advantage – you can – if permitted by your university regulations – write in the first person singular in your interpretivist project. Here the 'trick' in securing a high mark is to be able to convince your examiners of the quality of your interpretation of the phenomenon that you have explored. How you successfully achieve this is by relating the same tools of literature and research methods we have mentioned in this book with a knowledgeable, well-crafted argument about your topic that motivates it and drives the direction of your written report. It is this argument – your personal opinion based on your knowledge of the topic – that will have motivated your interest in learning about the organization you love; and the way that you introduce your knowledge from your reading and research to support this argument will produce a powerful story about your topic that will persuade the examiners of the quality of your project.

Many business school students in and beyond the UK have been asked to omit their 'I' in their research and write-up in the interest of 'objectivity'. This is considered by some researchers to be a serious error in studying the behaviour of organizations and their managers as failing to acknowledge the role of the researcher also fails to appreciate the fundamentally personal, intepretivist world of management in organizations that is founded on the subjective preferences of individuals and not on the objects of their actions or activities (for example, on performance and other outcomes that are 'objectively' measured).

Accordingly, if your research is about the management of people in organizations and you are interested in the behaviour of organizational actors, then your examiners' criteria of judgement will be the extent to which you have been able to articulate and systematically engage your argument to make sense of your data and produce a well-informed story of your research, supported by good data that answers your RQ.

If, on the other hand, you are studying an organization's financial performance, productivity, and other output phenomena where results need to be tested and explanations deduced, then you would need to use suitable, 'objective' language for presenting your research in the third person. This approach presumes the neutrality of the researcher; and in this scenario students adopting a mixed language – language that confuses methodologies – may be marked down. Students need therefore to carefully match methodologies and methods.

While research methods (research tools) may be mixed, one of the most typical errors that students make is to say they will adopt a research design with 'mixed methodologies'. We would severely caution against trying to adopt mixed methodologies. Drawing on our holiday analogy, this would be similar to having a dual view of your dream holiday in which you would seek to lie on the beach while also soldiering in the TA. Clearly, this makes no sense.

In business research projects, regardless of whether you adopt a positivist or interpretivist epistemology, you therefore start your project with an opening set of beliefs about the nature of the phenomenon of your study.

A key difference between the two epistemologies is that in a positivist study you will then wish to seek confirmation or rejection of hypotheses which you have tested, while interpretivist researchers will be interested in exploring elements of the chosen phenomena, some of which may have emerged from the research (for example, the management styles of top executives in a project about the decision-making processes in your chosen organization).

However, in both epistemologies, the use of different tools for conducting positivist and interpretivist research is united by a prior interest in addressing a well formed RQ (see pages 16 to 18 above); and by the same need to present a powerful, convincing explanation of the phenomenon under study.

In this explanation, the researcher's personal preferences – as shown in her choice of ontology and epistemology – and her argument(s) will drive the strength of the story presented about the topic and persuade her audience to also believe that the story that claims to explain the phenomenon is plausible and acceptable to them.

Let us illustrate what we have said with an example of the effects of differences between a positivist and an interpretivist approach to your research.

Our example here is taken from a case study of business change in a 120-year-old, fourth-generation family firm in Singapore that we have named 'Sinocare' (Ng and Keasey, 2010). In the case, the dominant conception of the family firm held by family shareholders changed very significantly from an orthodox and inflexible view of the family-owned and managed firm to a highly adaptable view of the family firm as a partnership among internal and external stakeholders. A major stimulus was a hostile but successful takeover by parties who sought to squeeze financial value from its assets by breaking up the firm.

If as a researcher you wished to study this period in the firm's development, what might be some immediate consequences for your research of the shift in the family's perception of the family firm?

RQ: Why Do Family Firms Persist?

Historical case study of family ownership and management over four generations

Throughout its 120-year history Sinocare had always been managed by blood relations of the founding family. This changed when the fourth-generation CEO took over in 1988 with a vision to grow the firm internationally. He believed that to achieve this would first require changing the controlling family's conception of the family firm. Under the old regime, family owners viewed their firm as a family-controlled entity in which its ownership was controlled by family members, while many of the firm's managers were also directly related to the share-owning family.

In this culture of family management, few non-family executives cared to join the firm, there remained a dearth of top management talent, and the customer base did not grow. For generations Sinocare went nowhere.

However, when the fourth-generation CEO sought to change the firm's conception of the family-owned and managed firm to one in which the family could prepare and promote non-family managers to the apex of the firm, then strong interest emerged from non-family managers, minority shareholders and financiers who had known the firm for many years but who had felt powerless to bring about cultural change. Strong support for this change became clear in the collaborative activities of stakeholders that were reflected in a new, broader, and non-nuclear conception of the family firm.

The nascent partnership between family and non-family stakeholders was put to the test in 1992 when the publicly quoted family firm was taken over by property developers whose principal interest was in developing its prime real estate. In response, Sinocare's family resolved to save the family business by 'working family members out of an executive role in the firm'. Very quickly the shareholding structure of the firm was reshaped to create a holding company for family shareholders, all family members were removed from executive roles in the former family-managed firm, and external financiers and other stakeholders were appointed to the board of directors. In place of the fourth-generation CEO a powerful group of non-family managers emerged who had been subordinated under the formal role of family managers.

This closely integrated group of internal and external stakeholders of the new Sinocare successfully wrested control of the firm from the property developers. Here, a change in perception of the family firm first by a key family manager and then by other major stakeholders had precipitated a transformation in the nature of the family-controlled firm. The stakeholder collaboration that was built on this changed conception subsequently altered Sinocare's fortunes in reversing a corporate takeover, and this saved the family business.

(Extract from Ng, W and Keasey, K (2010) 'Growing beyond smallness: how do small, closely-controlled firms survive?' *International Small Business Journal*, 28(6), pp 620–30)

Now if you as a researcher were studying, say, the business strategy of Sinocare before the firm's takeover in 1992 you might have formed an RQ that examined what the family firm's relationships were with its customers, competitors and other external, non-family stakeholders. This was because the family firm was treated by its controlling shareholders as a homogeneous entity of family owners and managers that changed little as the shareholding family kept tight control of ownership and management.

But, in the light of the takeover, if you also examined Sinocare's business strategy post-1992 then it would be extremely difficult not to develop an RQ that sought to find out how various family members conceived of their role in the firm post-takeover and how far non-family members actually played an influential role in the 'new' firm.

Accordingly, while an objectivist-positivist approach to research was possible in the stable and unchanging pre-1992 scenario of family control of their firm, we suggest that the fluid picture of business strategy following the takeover supported a constructionist-interpretivist research stance that examined changing conceptions of the family firm. Academic researchers should therefore appreciate how different research environments and circumstances may produce different research methodologies. In the case, this arose from a change in conception by family shareholders of their role in the family firm.

What has methodology got to do with research methods?

Drawing on the above case, let us now recap our advice on conceptualizing your research and move on to suggest how you may plan your research – plan for the journey you want to undertake – in more concrete terms.

In the following pages we raise a list of 'things to do' in planning your research, and the point of doing so is for you to make initial decisions on the strategic direction of your research.

The following chapters in Part 2, '"Doing" your project', will then put these decisions into operation by taking you step by step through each part of the research process as you conduct your research.

First, we believe we need to raise and 'put to bed' the phenomenon of quantitative versus qualitative research that seems to occupy the minds of many student researchers.

As illustrated in the above case, the popular distinction in research between either a qualitative or a quantitative conception of research is not useful for researchers of small student projects. Moreover, a conception of research as either qualitative or quantitative can prove very confusing for undergraduate and postgraduate students who are approaching their research project as a new and possibly one-off exercise. One reason is that qualitative and quantitative research are not the only research methodologies.

There are a number of research methodologies of which qualitative and quantitative are just two, and by referring to either qualitative or quantitative approaches to your research you may:

- miss out on popular methodologies that may be better suited than either a qualitative or quantitative approach, for example in researching a phenomenon such as leadership where ethnomethodology may be suitable; and
- fail to understand the core distinction between research methodologies and methods and confuse the deductive approach of quantitative methodology with the inductive perspective of qualitative studies.

Accordingly, while we discuss similarities and differences between qualitative and quantitative research and offer advice on developing each methodology as a distinct approach to your research, we ask you not to dwell on these conceptions as offering you a black and white view of research where you concentrate your energies on deciding whether your research is quantitative or qualitative and then forget what motivated you to pursue your research in the first place and what you want to learn.

Instead, we suggest that what is more important for undergraduate and MBA/MSc students than deciding whether your project is qualitative or quantitative is to decide firstly on the research stance that best reflects your personal beliefs, as we have suggested on page 26 above, and thereafter to develop and articulate a suitable, motivating RQ (pages 16–18 above). Both these activities form part of the same initial process of planning for your journey of research.

Another reason why we have suggested it may be confusing for you to think of your project as either qualitative or quantitative is that it is in fact common in many research projects to include both qualitative and quantitative research methods – called mixed methods – in a single research methodology.

So, for example, you might conduct a number of (qualitative) interviews and engage a (quantitative) method of correlating results from interview responses. We offer an actual example of a mixed methods research design within a qualitative methodology on pages 59–61 below.

Using mixed research methods is therefore not only possible, it is in many instances to be encouraged in order to strengthen your data analysis and produce rich findings (please note that quantitative research methods do not merely refer to statistics and numbers, as a popular – and mistaken – view held by some students suggests). However, having read and digested our advice we hope you understand that what we have been presenting to you is your research stance that you should make a decision on before you proceed in your research and that failing to make this decision may destabilize your entire project and cause examiners to question whether it should pass.

Specifically, we have urged you to decide on your research stance based on either an objectivist-positivist or a constructivist-interpretivist perspective. This is the first major decision you must make in your research as the decision on your research stance may then prompt you towards a suitable research methodology (for example, constructivist=>qualitative, or objectivist=>quantitative) and research methods.

As in the above case, it makes no sense to adopt a mixed research stance (objectivist *and* constructivist!). Students should therefore avoid any attempt to do so as this will produce confusing and un-researchable RQs.

For example, in our case above you might be grappling with how the controlling family conceived of the 'family firm', which is a constructivist RQ that would make little sense in the circumstances of the family's loss of control of the firm and its takeover, instead of what the performance of the family firm might have been during the years of family control, which may be a suitable positivist question for students' research in a small business project. We develop our advice on research methods, including mixed research methods that are popular with many students, on pages 50–69 below.

How may I design my research?

Once you have decided on your research stance and articulated your RQ, the next step is to structure a research design. Structuring a research design takes you beyond planning your journey of research (or deciding where to go and what to do) to the stage of preparing to embark on it (how you are going to get there and what to bring with you):

Planning your journey

Research stance (ontology and epistemology)

Preparing to leave

Research design and RQ (research methodology and methods)

In choosing a suitable methodology, its ability to answer your RQ will be your first consideration: a methodology is the specific research pathway that you will take to seek the answer to your question. For example, in our case above, in addressing the question 'Why do family firms persist?' a historical case methodology was adopted in which the issue of family control and management was traced over the 120-year lifespan of a long-lived family firm.

A research design is a framework for researching your project, and a design comprises a research methodology and (typically) a number of research methods.

A methodology offers a practical structure for conducting your research based on your ontological and epistemological beliefs.

You should note here that our methodology was a historical case study of family ownership and management. Given the extreme popularity of case study design among research students (and professional researchers), we discuss on pages 46–50 below the nature of case studies and how you may plan to use them correctly in a way that will set you up for your research and gain you appropriate credit.

By contrast with your research methodology, research methods comprise a collection of tools from which you make a selection for the purpose of collecting and analysing your project data. Given that research methods are tools, the methods you use need not be closely aligned to your chosen methodology. The point of research methods is for you to collect as much (quantitative) data or as rich (qualitative) data as possible, and in doing so we have already said that mixed research methods should be encouraged if this helps you achieve your objective of collecting quantity and/or quality of data and of analysing the data robustly (meaning systematically and thoroughly).

In practice, professional researchers have tended to prefer to use certain research methods with certain methodologies. For example, in our above case, as qualitative researchers we chose unstructured conversations as our chief research method. However, these 'intuitive' preferences should not limit your choice of research methods given the purpose of these tools we have just discussed. We offer a further discussion of how you may plan to include suitable research methods in your research design on pages 50–69 below.

In forming a suitable research design, your research stance will therefore lead you to choose a research methodology and research methods that follow from your research stance. Where your research stance sets out the basis for your project on a drawing board, your research design will then enable you to operationalize your project – which means to put it into operation once you've planned it. At this stage, at the level of an undergraduate and postgraduate small business project we do not believe you need to make another decision by selecting a research methodology from an array of methodologies.

Instead, for most students who wish to get started with their research, we suggest that you should assume that a positivist research stance is compatible with a largely quantitative methodology, while an interpretivist stance is consistent with a largely qualitative structure for your research. We say 'largely' as few research designs have been used in an exclusively quantitative or qualitative way, and we have already said that high-scoring student projects are able to 'mix' research methods by incorporating one or more qualitative methods in a quantitative design; and vice versa.

In a largely quantitative methodology we would suggest a 'cross-sectional' design involving one or more surveys or observations of your chosen sample of people at a single point in time. 'Cross section' therefore is about your study of a subset of a population that you believe 'represents' its behaviour in your area of study. For example, drawing from our travel analogy, a small cross-sectional study of the purpose of travel of UK citizens to a single destination – for example, to Siberia – during winter might involve posing this question to all UK citizens applying for a Russian visa in London on a few dates in winter.

The following section sets out details of two of the most popular research methods for you to gain an initial understanding of what research methods involve. The point here is to enable you to plan well for the next stage of operationalizing your research when, having made choices on your methodology and methods, you 'get into the field' and do your research.

How should I use my 'case study'?

An extremely popular methodology that many students like is a 'case study' research design. Although we wish to support your use of this methodology, we want to also encourage you to use it in a way that will produce rich data and findings for your project. Accordingly, to begin using the term productively we have placed 'case study' in quotation marks as students usually misconceive this term. First, a case study requires a specific phenomenon to be studied. This study is focused on addressing the RQ(s) at the heart of that study.

In our travel example above, a case study might be about the phenomenon of UK citizens who travel to Siberia during winter. Here your case forms a basic approach to your investigation of a single organization, entity or group of people or things. As the single case approach is by far the most popular form of research design for student projects at an undergraduate and postgraduate level, this puts pressure on you to be able to develop an RQ that can be addressed by data from your case.

In brief, it only makes sense to research your favourite organization for your project if you can obtain sufficient relevant data that can help you answer your RQ. (It is worth noting here that the most common chain stores in the UK are unlikely to cooperate with student projects if you do not already have access. Most are overwhelmed by such requests and refuse on principle! Remember that you must obtain permission from any organization before you submit your proposal.) While this runs true of all research, in choosing a single case you will have presumed that your case is an important example of the phenomenon of your study. You should keep a balance between the phenomenon you wish to study and your case where you choose to illustrate and illuminate features of that phenomenon with data from your case. Again you should be able to see this 'fit' by following the steps we have outlined in Chapters 2 and 3 for conceiving and planning your project. Otherwise, presuming without convincing reasons why you have chosen your case will not endear you to your examiners. Simply choosing a case on the basis of your personal preferences is not a sensible way to score a high mark in your project module!

Your single case study explores the intricate and particular nature of the research topic of your interest, and your findings from your study would therefore be drawn on to address your RQ of this phenomenon. Second, a case study is a methodology and not a research method. This means that you will still need to select and use one or more research methods (see the following chapter) to collect data, and this data may take either a more quantitative or a more qualitative dimension.

Many business project students have been unaware that case studies may be used in a quantitative way and not just in a qualitative research design. If your case study has a more quantitative dimension then you would be examining a large and representative sample within your case firm. Whether your case study has a more quantitative or a more qualitative dimension depends wholly on your RQ. If, for example, you wish to examine possible relationships between various strategies and firm performance in your case organization then your focal interest in relationships between variables will require a quantitative-led approach. A popular variation of this same theme is where you research a number of operations and locations of a single organization. To research these interests you will seek to collect as much data as possible on each of your variables, and your work plan here may be highly structured. A popular research tool to carry out a structured work plan is described under 'structured interview' on pages 56–58 below.

Furthermore, case designs are rarely just quantitative or qualitative.

As we also explain in the following section, elements of both, if used well, can significantly strengthen your case design. We suggest that you adopt at the outset of your research either a quantitative-led design or a qualitative-led design based on your RQ. Students in our experience have typically plumped for a qualitative-led design on the premise that they wish to conduct an 'in-depth' study, and this means their study will be qualitative. Please rethink this. We suggest below why 'in-depth' is a misleading term in research.

At this point we want to invite you to focus on the RQ that you should have developed.

Looking at this RQ, can you say if you are interested in:

- examining or assessing relationships between variables such as strategies and performance in our example above; or

- exploring corporate strategies or performance of your favourite organization as distinct phenomena; and/or

- understanding these phenomena, for example by learning the views of a group of employees in your case organization?

A well-known example of a quantitative-led case study design is Geert Hofstede's (1980) study of cultural dimensions within the IBM group of companies in 40 locations around the world. While working for IBM the author administered and analysed a vast number of questionnaires to IBM employees on attitudes, preferences and perceptions related to their work. Hofstede analysed responses that proved pertinent to his model of cultural 'dimensions' by defining and applying a standard questionnaire to measure culturally specific values in IBM worldwide. Although the author accepted that responses to a standard questionnaire should also be viewed qualitatively and not merely quantitatively, he focused on categorizing culture under distinct scores on standardized scales.

By contrast with the typically large samples of quantitative projects (we suggest a 'rule-of-thumb' sample size below), in carrying out a qualitative case study of a phenomenon, you should set out to explore your phenomenon among a small number of interviewees, or respondents as many qualitative researchers who conduct informal conversations instead of formal interviews like to call their interviewees. Your RQ in a qualitative case design of a small business project would normally focus on the nature of a single phenomenon:

as a rule of thumb you have no time and space to properly explore multiple phenomena.

For example, in developing our example above you might ask: What is the nature of corporate strategy in a contemporary, high-technology organization?

In addressing this RQ you may choose a qualitative case study of high technology in your favourite organization. However, in embarking on your research and speaking to people in your organization you might discover unexpected themes of interest that you may not be able to immediately relate with your original phenomenon of interest but which are nonetheless interesting. This journey of discovery that leads you to gather data on and explore unplanned themes of interest is a typical feature of qualitative case studies, and we have already offered an example of a qualitative case on pages 39–40 above.

Both quantitative and qualitative approaches to case studies have their own dedicated research methods, as we will describe below, but a key difference between the two approaches is in the large sample (representativeness) of quantitative case studies compared with the principal interest of qualitative cases in exploring the perceptions of the researcher's phenomenon held by a relatively small number of primary respondents.

Here we should explain why the difference in the two approaches to case studies is not one of 'in-depth' study. As all case studies and all interviews for cases are 'in-depth' we would suggest omitting this term that may be taken to mean that only qualitative case studies are 'in-depth' and therefore, by implication, useful. This implication is incorrect! Instead, we would suggest that student researchers using case studies focus only on their RQ when developing a case study design that may yield primarily quantitative or primarily qualitative data that best address their question. This decision should not be difficult if you have taken our advice on your research stance as your decision on how to structure and develop your case study follows from your personal ontology and epistemology.

For example, a small number of students we have supervised – largely those intending to progress to doctoral studies – have adopted an experimental design (a largely quantitative approach to research that involves setting up two or more groups of people – their student colleagues – whose behaviour is then manipulated, as in a laboratory experiment). More often however an ethnographic methodology (a largely qualitative form of case study over time of specific cultural phenomena – from the Greek *ethnos* for 'people' – of the researcher's interest) has been preferred to laboratory experiments in order to engage with 'real world' phenomena.

Each of these methodologies has its own framework for business research. In experimental research, quantitative relationships are tested between experimental and control groups, while in ethnographic cases, behaviour is studied in actual situations – for example, in exploring the buying behaviour of a targeted group of consumers (see Peñaloza, 1994) – or the characteristics and needs of an under-privileged population in highly focused, long-term studies (Hill, 2001). In collecting their data, experimental researchers and ethnographers may draw from the same 'tool chest' of research methods as all other methodologies, with a small number of exceptions where, for example, ethnographers have developed internet-based virtual methods and video methods for collecting data in their natural settings (see Hine, 2008).

What research methods should I use for my project?

The term 'research methods' is often used as a catch-all term to include all aspects of a research process, from choosing your research stance to developing your research design and collecting and analysing your data. To target as clinically as possible what you have to do at each stage of your research, we present research methods as your chosen means – your usable and effective tools – for collecting data.

Typically your initial questions on research methods would be about how to put into practice a very limited range of tools that many students seem to have gotten into their minds are the only tools that satisfy the rubric of 'primary research'.

Here you might ask:

- What research tools should I use – and develop my knowledge of – for my project?

- How may I choose suitable research methods?
- How may I understand research methods well enough for me to apply them?

Typically you would use surveys and interviews in the belief that surveys would be used as a major tool of both quantitative and qualitative studies, while interviews in your view might serve as a qualitative tool to garner 'in-depth' data on your phenomenon (I have already suggested that as interviews are always in-depth this term is unnecessary).

Following your decision on your case study, your next major decision should be to select research methods that will enable you to address your RQ. As that RQ guides your methods, please ensure that the data you propose to collect actually allow you to address your RQ! Again this isn't difficult if you've conceptualized your research by making the prior decisions we have suggested on your research stance (see page 26 above).

An example of a popular research method: surveys

Of the many tools in quantitative and qualitative research, surveys are by far the most commonly used in both types of research. Many undergraduate and postgraduate students, however, develop superficial and poorly thought-through surveys that suggest little knowledge of, and consideration for, using this tool. Just as in designing case studies, many students have also mistakenly viewed surveys as only applicable in quantitative research. In fact, surveys can be used for either quantitative or qualitative research.

A survey involves you developing and despatching a questionnaire in which cross-sectional data are obtained (please note that the word data is always plural!). Recall here that cross-sectional data concern respondents' views that were obtained at the particular moment in time when the data were collected.

Typically, questionnaires may be delivered electronically to a large number of respondents as your 'hit rate' – or rate of return from your questionnaires – is likely to be low. As a 5–10 per cent return for random questionnaires is an average you might reasonably expect (unless you are sending questionnaires to friends and other known samples, or if you can secure access to and assistance from a top company executive or executives to chase subordinates for you, which is as difficult a task as it sounds), then for your small business project you should aim to e-mail at least 500 possible respondents.

As a university student you may increase your number of responses if you play smart by engaging with, and sending questionnaires to, stakeholders in your university community (see page 58 below), either exclusively or as part of your coverage of the types of respondents you require.

Although it is impossible to offer any definite answer to one of the most common questions from students – 'How large should my sample be?' – because every project has different time, cost and other constraints, in our experience of small student projects we believe that for quantitative projects 50 responses to a small survey would produce a minimum amount of data that can be worked with to produce convincing findings.

As a general indicator, in quantitative projects the bigger your sample the better the validity of your quantitative project – and potentially also the higher your project mark if you can build on your sample size in your statistical tests. The principal reason why in quantitative research a large sample is always better than a small sample is simple: the absolute size of any sample matters, and not its relative size to your chosen (or any other) population.

As a rule, the larger the size of a sample, the more precise the sample is likely to be when you are generalizing from your particular sample, say, of consumers to the total population of consumers.

Conversely, small samples will contribute to the persistence of significant sampling errors, which will normally diminish in proportion to sample size: generally, the larger the size of your sample, the smaller the number of sampling errors. In quantitative research, you should aim to achieve as low as possible sampling errors, as an important objective of your research is that its results should be reliable. Low sampling errors therefore increase the reliability of your results. In turn, reliable findings support the validity of your research as a whole, while high validity will always mean a high project mark (see Chapter 10: Analysing quantitative data).

In trying to achieve reliability and validity in quantitative projects, your survey questions and answers should therefore be set up in a standard format so that subsequently you can feed your data into statistical tests. To do so you must see that every multiple-choice answer is presented in a simple format where the same words are used as far as possible as the basis for answers to each question. Simple formats also have the valuable benefit of increasing the attractiveness of your questionnaire for respondents while simplifying your process of data collation and analysis.

For qualitative projects a respondent sample smaller than 50 will normally be acceptable: a) if respondents provide additional, written or tape-recorded comments beyond making single choices from multiple-choice answers; and b) where your survey responses provide a basis for you to conduct a number of interviews with respondents (whether individually or in groups) to follow up answers given by respondents and to gain deeper understanding of themes that are merely introduced by survey questions.

The following are specific steps for you to take in planning suitable research methods. These steps apply in both quantitative and qualitative cases of small student projects. Our advice assumes you have no special access to a sample of respondents or interviewees, and that we are looking to help you generate the highest possible returns and fullest possible answers to your questions. Your follow-on chapters below (pages 85–152) will take you step by step through the process of developing and implementing your chosen research methods for your project:

1. Before you begin your research, develop a list of target respondents – what types of respondents (for example, student, manager, executive) and what role each group performs, instead of just the names and e-addresses of respondents.

This is a first, important step in securing a reasonable chance of a 5–10 per cent return in a questionnaire. We suggest you ask yourself two key questions to help you think realistically about obtaining a sufficiently large and varied amount of project data, as outlined above. First, what internet resources can you draw on to reach your desired audience? Think of all the social media channels where you imagine your target respondents may have a presence, such as

LinkedIn, in addition to Facebook and Twitter. Second, think creatively about how you might approach possible respondents without publicly posting a mass email that would rarely attract much attention. For example, you might start a blog – just as many of our project students have typically started blogs – about a public event that your target company has recently been involved in, post a few opinionated comments from your friends on social media and then invite your recipients to respond. This approach tries to exploit some people's curiosity in learning about and discussing events that they are also interested and/or involved in.

Remember that as no research method is guaranteed to produce data you will continually have to be imaginative to look for additional sources for data, for example, in and around your workplace and home.

2. Start developing your questionnaire by breaking down your RQ into many small questions that may be answered independently of one another but which are related to one another in your research.

A clear, motivating RQ gives you a helpful basis for developing data-gathering questions on distinct aspects of your RQ. For example, if we return to our travel analogy, a principal RQ for a business researcher who seeks to explore the holiday choices of potential customers for a boutique travel agency might be: 'How far do free independent travellers from the UK choose a beach holiday over an adventure holiday?'

As this RQ involves a primarily quantitative approach (the question 'how far' normally suggests a comparative analysis of a large dataset), your main data for addressing this RQ can easily be broken down into a number of sub-questions based on various themes in this RQ.

For example, you will see at least three distinct themes in the RQ we have suggested above:

- free independent travellers;
- beach holidays; and
- adventure holidays.

Other themes that might be used in your questionnaire include the UK origin of travellers mentioned in the RQ, and underlying conceptions of the nature of holidays among employed professionals in and beyond the UK and other Western economies.

Set up each of these three themes as questions, using open-ended words to begin your questions, namely, what, why, when and how.

Avoid closed-ended questions that require yes or no answers.

Even if you believe the world is black and white, asking your respondents to give a yes or no answer to questions where yes or no answers are difficult (we believe that most questions in business are tough to provide a clear answer to) will not help you achieve your principal objective of a large number of high-quality returns.

Accordingly, even in surveys for quantitative projects, begin a majority of your questions with what, why, when, and how. Then provide a multiple choice of four plausible answers for each question. More than four answers might again hinder you from obtaining the largest possible number of high-quality returns (an exception here is if you set up a Likert scale for some of your questions, as described below and on pages 95–96).

3. Set up interesting, direct questions.

To draw up your four possible answers above will require you to be knowledgeable about your chosen industry and organization(s). Here we suggest that you draw up answers by imagining yourself as a respondent to your own questions: What are plausible and practical answers that you might think of for each question? For student researchers in their first project it would be useful for you to work with a colleague to develop a wider range of possible answers, with each of you alternately posing a question and possible answers to each other.

At the end of each set of plausible answers remember to provide an empty box for alternative answers and any comments – which could be very precious to you, as discussed above. In many student and non-student projects, comments in just a few boxes – or very occasionally even one relevant comment – have provided insights for researchers to develop powerful, convincing explanations for their RQs. In business projects, as you are studying people who practise business in the area of your interest, you are trying to get into the minds of business people typically to make sense of and explain their behaviour and/or the outcomes of their business activities, for example, in terms of their company's performance.

An additional way to glean a large number of brief, structured answers to direct questions in a questionnaire is by asking for respondents' views of a specific event or topic (normally set up as a statement) and by then offering (usually) five possible answers on a scale of high agreement to disagreement with the statement. This Likert scale (named after its inventor) is the most widely used means of rating responses in survey questionnaires and requires researchers to set up prior, multiple-choice views of a statement. If your statement is clearly articulated and the five responses to the statement cover a full range of possible opinions, then you may get answers that could be used as a preliminary measure of responses to your statement. As with all your questions in your questionnaire, your Likert-scale statements should also relate with and help you answer one or more parts of your RQ.

However, using a Likert scale in an effective way depends on your being able to obtain a large number of returns for your questionnaire where you can then scale responses based on each of your five possible responses. The larger the number of returns, the more useful your Likert scale will be in supporting your respondents' view of a statement.

Just using a Likert scale will not gain you extra marks in your project unless: a) you show how your scale relates to your research design; and b) you have a sufficient number of returns that you can then process and use in a clear way to strengthen some aspect of your story.

As with a minimum number of survey responses and interviews for your project, there is no set threshold for the number of responses you need. We believe you will know when you have sufficient responses for your Likert scale to work as this is a quantitative tool that you are using, for example, to support or refute direct statements. Instead of wondering whether or not you have a sufficient number of responses, ask yourself: How confident are you that the responses to your Likert statements give you a clear view of your respondents' opinions? Bear in mind that 'clear' simply means that you are able to get a clear idea of the opinions of your respondents and does not necessarily mean that you have obtained definitive answers to any statement.

Likert scales are regarded by researchers as a closed-ended research tool in that they present a closed set of answers. As with your interviews we do not believe it is useful for you to view your Likert scale as a closed mechanism that will produce closed answers. Instead, it is much more important to develop a research design where it is clear how your Likert data contribute significantly to it. On pages 59–61 we offer an example of how we have used a Likert scale to strengthen the research design of an actual project by integrating our Likert scale with unstructured interviews in a qualitative research design of a project which we reported in a recently published journal article.

4. Combine your survey with a structured interview in a quantitative project or with a semi-structured or unstructured interview in qualitative research.

In quantitative projects, you could, for instance, undertake say three or four structured interviews of 30 minutes each with your contacts before you post your questionnaire.

The point of these structured interviews would be to help you develop and refine your survey questions. Your structured interviews may therefore be used as a pilot study (meaning a small exploratory study to assess if your project can be researched) to improve your survey, given that your survey is your main tool for generating as many responses as possible. Developing and refining your survey questions in this way will reduce the trial-and-error nature of building these questions in a first-time research project. Another important reason for structured interviews is to help you gain better understanding of your industry and organization(s), which will then feed into a more informed interpretation of your findings in your write-up.

Structured interviews require you to administer:

- identical questions;
- delivered in an identical order; and as far as possible in the same timeframe;
- to all interviewees by reading a preamble and interview questions from a prepared paper.

The objective of structured interviewing is for you to acquire enough data that may be aggregated, for example so that you can run statistical tests to first chart, and then verify, similarities and differences in responses.

Accordingly, in structured interviews you stick to questions you prepared before each interview, and a successful set of interviews would be where you are able to replicate all interviews in the same manner and not to conduct interviews that are adapted to circumstances. The point here is to try and obtain as standard a format as possible for your answers across all your interviews so that they may be comparable.

To achieve this you will conduct just one interview for each interviewee, unless you decide to administer two interviews per interviewee, for example if you wish to conduct an examination of any changes in your interviewees' views over a certain length of time. Deviation from a standard format in interviews and surveys that you have set in your own quantitative research design should be avoided.

In terms of respondents and interviewees, examples of easy-to-access research samples in a university setting are your fellow students, who could be regarded as a principal resource for you, university lecturers in and beyond your department, and department and university administrators. This last group is often neglected despite the fact that they are also stakeholders in your university, while administrators may also have distinctive preferences from students and lecturers. Apart from these internal stakeholders, other members of a university community include important external stakeholders such as alumni and alumnae, suppliers and service providers, and also potential students and staff. In short, in a typical university in and beyond Europe and the United States you have a potentially rich and full community of interest groups who represent large and important sections of your total population of consumers, stakeholders etc. You need to select and engage with these groups by surveying them on a topic in which they have a strong interest. Also, you may need permission to e-mail staff/administrators and may not have access to external e-mail lists such as for suppliers etc without your survey being vetted first for content and grammar.

Importantly, for quantitative projects university communities can provide a data sample that is representative of many target populations, and students undertaking quantitative research may with little difficulty engage with stakeholders from their university community in developing a representative sample of their target population in their specific field of interest.

For example, in following on and developing your research on travel destinations of free and independent travellers (FIT) (see page 54 above), you may draw data from a representative sample in your university that includes:

- FIT customers (alumni and alumnae in managerial roles);

- non-FIT customers (your student colleagues!);

- semi-FIT customers; and

- specialist knowledge providers (relevant lecturers), suppliers to the tourism and hospitality industry (relevant university departments and external stakeholders such as book publishers), and marketing, media and communications administrators in and/or attached to your university who would understand the administrative and operational aspects of managing a business with a high level of customer interface, as in your travel project.

In brief, in a typical university community you have a microcosm of many segments of society that you can conveniently draw from in setting up a representative quantitative sample that is acceptable to your examiners.

A project combining a survey and structured interviews

Let us now illustrate our advice by suggesting how you may develop a research design that combines two research methods, a survey and structured interviews, in a small business project. We have chosen this example specifically to suggest how quantitative research methods may be used in a qualitative research design. The excerpt is drawn from a recently published journal article by Wilson Ng and other colleagues.

Mixed-Methods Research in Exploring Customer
Profiles of Four Retail Businesses

In this project the authors drew on customer questionnaires
and structured interviews with company managers of four retail
businesses in a qualitative research design. Our RQ was this: How
have small, high street family businesses in advanced European
economies continued to compete and thrive? Specifically, we wanted to learn
how intuitive perception between managers and customers may be used by
four businesses (two family firms and two non-family firms). In addressing our
RQ we applied an original statistical model to assess the degree of intuitive
perception between managers and customers of each business.

We tackled our RQ in two parts. First (RQ1), we assessed the degree
of concordance between the perceptions of senior managers and repeat
customers of each of the four businesses. For RQ1 we interviewed top
managers of all four businesses. Based on these interviews we developed
questionnaires for customers of each business. We then administered
the questionnaires over 12 months to customers in the four stores where
each of the businesses were located. This time frame was used to control
for seasonality. The results of the questionnaires were analysed with a
statistical 'perceptive concordance index' or 'PCI'. This PCI was applied
to over 100 customers of each of the stores, and the usable returns were
obtained from a total of over 400 customers. With this number of returns
we were able to engage two research methods in a quantitative way
to satisfactorily address RQ1, which was about assessing the proximity
between the views of senior managers and those of repeat customers.

In addressing RQ2, another statistical method was used to assess
and support our PCI results by exploring if there was a causal effect
between those results and the particular nature of the firm as a family-
owned or non-family-owned entity. The rationale for using this probability
method was to assess the relationship between the nature of the firm
and customers' preference for buying from the outlets in which they were
surveyed. Data from our PCI supported by the results of this assessment
comprised the body of findings, which we then interpreted. In this second
part of our research (RQ2), we interpreted our findings by relating them
to our knowledge of the literatures on intuitive perception and tacit
knowledge.

Data collection

In collecting data for our research we interviewed owner-managers of two
family-owned firms, and senior managers of each of the two non-family
stores. All managers were interviewed individually for approximately an

hour and a half each. Owner-managers of one of the family firms were the four brothers who run the business. Each of the brothers is responsible for a different area of the business, although each of the brothers reported that the views of all four brothers carry equal weight. The second family firm's owner-managers were two brothers and a sister who also reported that their respective views carry equal weight. In the non-family stores the two managers were the top personnel responsible for managing, respectively, the bakery and the bookstore.

All interviews were structured, with a headline protocol of two key issues followed by 13 sub-questions that followed directly from each of the issues. These issues were, first, that we sought to learn what each top manager thought to be the strengths and weaknesses of their business. Second, we wanted to know how managers of the four businesses communicated with (which of) their customers. We obtained further information about how each business perceived its own strengths from secondary data, principally company websites and brochures. A profile of the strengths and weaknesses of each business was then drawn from our interviews and secondary data.

With these profiles to hand we developed customer questionnaires for each of the four firms. Each questionnaire contained nine questions on customers' views of the business that they were patronizing at the time of our questionnaire. Following questions on gender etc to draw a general profile of each respondent, the core part of the questionnaire asked respondents to indicate their frequency of purchases in other stores and how far their choice of store had been influenced by its specific features. These features comprised the business strengths that were mentioned earlier by managers. For each feature we allotted a value on a Likert scale with five modalities: 1 (no influence); 2 (little influence); 3 (a reason for my choice); 4 (a principal reason for my choice); and 5 (the only reason for my choice).

Data analysis

With interview and survey data to hand, we coded interviews and survey data from the four businesses using an open-source program for statistical computation that has been widely used as reference software. Coded data were manually ordered on the basis of the perceived strengths of each business. The degree of concordance between perceptions was then assessed by applying our PCI and by using the measures on the Likert scales as indicative measures for each value we set up for customers and managers of the four businesses.

(Extract from Dessi, C, Ng, W, Floris, M and Cabras, S (in press) How small family businesses may compete through tacit knowledge, *Journal of Small Business and Enterprise Development*, 14(5), pp 673–94)

The most popular research method: qualitative interviews

As in our example above, in qualitative projects interviews are an important means for you as a researcher to develop understanding of the themes of your research. This understanding will then form a principal basis for you to address your RQ.

As with quantitative research you are generating and collecting data for your research, with your respondents and interviewees providing your raw material in the form of data for you to analyse and to make sense of (interpret) in developing answer(s) to your RQ, which would then complete your story.

However, beyond these similarities, interviews in qualitative projects have fundamental differences in approach, objectives and content with their quantitative counterparts. First, in qualitative research we would suggest that you conduct most of your interviews *following* your survey.

Your survey will then provide a basis for your interviews by helping you to develop and refine interview questions that may best capture the data you want. For example, as qualitative interviews focus on the interviewee's perspective(s), your survey may suggest areas of interest for discussion and topics for you to probe with interviewees as to why they may be of greater or lesser interest to them. (By contrast in structured interviews for quantitative projects, you may 'test' standard questions on a small sample of interviewees before attempting to standardize your questions in a survey questionnaire for a larger number of respondents.)

Let us return again to our FIT research. Suppose that you develop your RQ into a qualitative project by focusing on the reasons why a sample of FIT travellers made their holiday choices. Following your initial survey of university students and other stakeholders you might conduct qualitative interviews of a few FIT alumni and alumnae. In getting to know their reasons you will want to learn as comprehensively as possible about the reasons they had for making their decisions on their holidays. You would therefore want your interviewees to talk about themselves as much as possible, and your survey would provide you with an initial guide, for example, of what they might like to talk about and their initial responses to questions that in an interview you may then choose to probe.

A typical approach to qualitative interviews suggests that these interviews may be conducted in a semi-structured or an unstructured format. A semi-structured interview means that you will prepare a few questions before your interview and you will start your interview by posing at least a few of these questions. However, you will leave plenty of room during the interview to explore any themes, subjects and ideas that are interesting to your interviewee and which typically emerge in the course of a good interview (see 'Collecting qualitative data' on pages 85–98).

In an unstructured conversation, your emphasis will be on the emergent aspect of the interview where you will seek to encourage your interviewee to talk in detail about her views in, around and beyond your initial subject. Your task in this unstructured conversation is precisely to engage your interviewee in extended conversation with you, and a successful interview is the extent to which you are able to get your interviewee to speak freely about themes, subjects and ideas that are of interest to her.

Your initial questions therefore act as a catalyst for a broad-ranging and detailed conversation between you and the interviewee. Here the point of qualitative interviewing in both semi-structured and unstructured formats is to generate high-quality, 'rich' data about your interviewee's views in and about a range of themes, subjects, and ideas. You will then seek to make sense of and interpret this data by drawing on your literature in a later part of your project report, in your Discussion principally, and also in your Conclusion (see Chapter 16).

A number of textbooks suggest that flexibility in the way that you design and administer interviews is important to gain good, rich data in qualitative interviews (see, for example, Bryman and Bell, 2011, pp 405–6). In your research methods classes you may also be asked to decide whether you wish to set up a semi-structured or unstructured interview format. Soon you begin to wonder about making yet another decision and end up opting, without much thought, for a semi-structured format of interviewing as a middle ground between what you might have been taught to perceive as the 'extreme' option of unstructured interviewing and a structured format which intuitively you might think will constrain your interview style and produce too little quality data.

However, few textbooks admit that learning to set up your interviews in a semi-structured or unstructured format isn't very useful for your research. In the practice of qualitative interviewing you won't actually find a great deal of difference between these two formats. This is because your focal interest should be on your interviewee (your conversation partner), and in qualitative research you want to learn her views and opinions in and beyond your topic in as much detail as possible.

Accordingly, as suggested on page 61 above, you may seek out your interviewees' perspectives of certain themes of your interest, but you should also be prepared to explore other themes of interest to your interviewees. The link here between planned and unplanned themes of conversation is in learning how your interviewees relate them. You then use theory to make sense of your interviewees' perspectives and develop a convincing answer to your RQ by weaving together multiple interviewees' perspectives.

To learn your interviewees' perspectives and how they may relate themes of their interest requires you to develop a keen interest in listening. We elaborate on how you may develop and use good listening skills in conducting your business research in Chapter 5, but in planning your research we want to get you started on thinking through what kind of listening skills you will need to develop as a qualitative researcher. We offer this advice in three discrete steps at the end of this chapter.

Few research books dwell on listening in qualitative research, possibly because listening is a 'soft' skill that can be hard to learn for novice and experienced researchers alike. Listening is hard partly because it requires the listener to concentrate not only on understanding what the interviewee is saying but also on trying to perceive what she is trying to say beyond her spoken words.

Listening therefore goes beyond mere hearing of spoken words and requires intuitive understanding of the interviewee's actual meaning. This dual function of listening is what makes qualitative interviewing tiring. The difficulty of listening well also has implications for your scheduling of qualitative interviews as you would be well advised to avoid conducting more than say three interviews of one and a half hours each in a day. Experienced qualitative interviewers would struggle with three interviews a day! As a novice interviewer, you have an additional, major burden in also having to concentrate on your own performance so that you can get high-quality data from your interview.

These limitations have a knock-on effect in the cost of qualitative interviews if you have to travel to your interview destinations. Bryman and Bell (2011) suggest that out-of-town researchers might consider conducting 'intensive interviews' (p 466) if they are operating on a tight budget by packing a large number of face-to-face interviews into a day. While you may be constrained by costs, this kind of approach to organizing interviews will not be effective in gaining high-quality data. Instead, a practical alternative might be to slightly redesign your research, for example so that you conduct your research in an organization that is more convenient for you to access over a period of time.

Alternatively, as we live in a technology age, Skype, teleconferencing and social media that are available on many university campuses may be used as alternative tools to communicate with interviewees. You may need to be more innovative than requesting a conventional face-to-face meeting to gain access to your interviewees (again see 'Collecting qualitative data').

Psychologists have suggested how being a good listener also requires the development of certain personality traits related to an ability to absorb and reflect on information that may be presented by people with personalities that clash with the interviewer's personality.

Can you resist setting out your own view of events or voicing your opinion in an interview? Here you need to appreciate that a qualitative interview for you to learn about your interviewees' perspectives is quite different from an interview conducted for example by Jeremy Paxman on *Newsnight* or David Letterman on his CBS show who typically end up debating with their interviewees. An important difference here is that while you should treat all your interviewees with respect, you are not the centre of attraction and should resist any attempt to impose yourself in your interview. If you are a novice researcher and/or if you have a dominant personality where you like to talk, this will take some changing.

Qualitative interviewing therefore is often extremely difficult. There are other research methods as we have described in this chapter, and you are not making a correct choice if you choose qualitative interviews because you think they are an easy or an obvious option. If you go down this path you are likely to end up with poor data. Even if you know a few people in your chosen organization and you believe they will give you good data, actually getting good data depends very largely on your listening and other related skills as an interviewer.

In fact, we believe that qualitative researchers should struggle to get good data as high-quality data are often co-created with interviewees.

This is to say that good qualitative researchers learn to manage their interviewees so that interviewees will use their interviews as a way to talk through their ideas. While this process isn't necessarily 'therapeutic' to interviewees, being encouraged to talk deeply about topics of their interest is perhaps one of the few attractive aspects of being interviewed for interviewees. It would be a nice achievement of a qualitative interview for interviewees to have an opportunity to talk openly about themselves where a talkative interviewee is often a good sign that the interview is going well and that you are getting good data.

Hard though it seems to conduct a good qualitative interview, there are a number of interview skills you can learn.

What exactly are these skills? Let us suggest a few that you should consider developing in order to obtain good data when you get into the field.

1. *Listening*. There is never a limit to developing or fine-tuning your listening skills. A prime objective in the following steps is for you to listen carefully to your interviewee so that you may pick up points in her narrative that are important to her and probe one or more of those points. A good listener keeps asking herself: Why is a particular point important to my interviewee and how might a point relate to her perspective of other points?

2. *Listening involves practice*. The first five or so minutes of a qualitative interview 'set the scene' for the interview, and

this 'preamble' can therefore be of crucial importance to its direction and the quality of data you subsequently get. Rehearsing the first few minutes of an interview in front of a mirror and a tape recorder can be very useful to try and ensure that you control as much as you can control at the outset of your interview. The objective here is to make crystal clear what you want to talk about so that you may give yourself a useful platform to engage with interviewees and get them to talk.

Talking at least initially about a) the objectives of your interview and b) headline themes or topics you have prepared for your interview will then help you in your process of data analysis; and with due preparation, you can get your interviewees to talk, using as a platform for conversation the initial themes you have outlined. After all, you can safely assume that your interviewees have agreed to be interviewed in order to help you!

3. *Prepare well and early for all interviews by researching: a) public and private profiles of and news about your interviewee; and b) news about your interviewee's organization.*

You already know that in our internet age a tremendous amount of information is available on just about anything. Your problem in fact will be that you have too much information to review and too little time in which to select and study pertinent websites. Much of this problem can be addressed by preparing for your project as early as possible. Preparing for interviews is an integral part of your project preparation. Here many students do not help themselves by starting work on their projects with only a little time left before submission. This kind of approach takes you even further away from developing a high-quality project.

4. *Decide on a very small number of chief contacts in your target organization and use these contacts as your principal source of data.*

This technique of collecting data from and through a few chief contacts in your case firm should be used in both small and large qualitative research projects as a practical way to collect high-quality data. Ask yourself: Who can best provide me the data I need for my project? Once you've established a chief contact or contacts then your principal relationship will be with these contacts. In small business projects, you will not normally need, or have the time, to develop additional contacts and relationships. While focusing on a chief contact requires you to make a careful choice, trying to gain access through a single contact can also serve as a way for you to explore the viability of your access to that organization; and if you make contact early enough in your project then you will have time to try and access another contact in another organization if you choose to or if you have to do so. We offer detailed advice on how to access organizations and use your contacts for your research on pages 58 and 121 onwards.

Of course you need to be realistic if your intention is to research a large organization whose CEO is your best source of data; but as many student projects we have supervised concern small and medium-sized businesses our suggested approach of relating with a chief contact seems both obvious and practical. Further, seasoned researchers usually start their research by thinking about what they need and then placing roles and names together as possible sources of data to meet each need. We recommend this approach to student researchers. If it isn't practical to interview your best interviewee then at that time consider the next best alternatives.

Some students (and seasoned researchers) have conducted their projects in a different way by interviewing people and organizations they know. While this approach isn't wrong we have already suggested that you may not obtain good data if you approach anyone without first developing a clear research design based on what you want to learn. Our belief is that in developing a high-quality qualitative project names of organizations and people follow this design, and not vice versa.

Our view is supported by the requirement in qualitative research to: a) rationalize your choice of organization; and b) generalize from your findings in your case to the industry in which your organization is located, and beyond to other industries outside your research context if this is feasible although you should see provisos in the following chapters about analysing your findings. All this would be easier if you develop a strong research design into which your organization and contacts fit without positioning a poorly thought-through design against your contacts and discover in your interviews that your contacts do not really suit your design.

In sum, in planning to obtain high-quality data from qualitative interviews, focus on choosing a suitable chief contact and then on preparing to listen as suggested to your interviewees.

Having conceptualized and planned your research you should now be ready to embark on your journey of research. So let's get into the field!

References

Bryman, A and Bell, E (2011) *Business Research Methods*, 3rd edn, Oxford University Press, Oxford

Denzin, N and Lincoln, Y (eds) (2003) *Collecting and Interpreting Qualitative Materials*, Sage, London

Dessi, C, Ng, W, Floris, M and Cabras, S (in press) How small family businesses may compete through tacit knowledge, *Journal of Small Business and Enterprise Development*, 14(5), pp 673–94

Hill, R (2001) Surviving in a material world: evidence from ethnographic consumer research on people in poverty, *Journal of Contemporary Ethnography*, 30(4), pp 364–391

Hine, C (2008) Virtual ethnography: modes, varieties, affordances in Fielding, N, Lee, R and Blank, G (eds) *The SAGE Handbook of Online Research Methods*, pp 257–270, Sage, London.

Hofstede, G (1980) *Culture's Consequences: International differences in work-related values*, Sage, Beverly Hills CA

Holstein, J and Gubrium, J (1995) *The Active Interview (Qualitative Research Methods)*, Sage, Thousand Oaks, CA

Ng, W and Keasey, K (2010) Growing Beyond Smallness: how do small, closely-controlled firms survive? *International Small Business Journal*, 28(6), pp 620–30

Peñalosa, L (1994) Atravesando fronteras/Border crossings: a critical ethnographic exploration of the consumer acculturation of Mexican immigrants, *Journal of Consumer Research*, 21(1), pp 32–54

PART TWO
'Doing' your project

03
The project proposal

The purpose of this chapter is to go through what is expected from a project proposal. A proposal is normally completed for projects some months before the full project is due in and can be assessed as part of the module. In any event, it is likely you will receive feedback from your supervisor as to how you can improve your project.

This chapter will cover what the component parts of a proposal are – the elements that you will be expected to cover. It is important not to think about the proposal just as an (assessment) element within a module, but as the preliminary project plan that proposes the topic that you wish to research and how you intend to undertake this research. It is important to make it as complete as possible and to have completed a significant amount of reading etc before tackling it.

In the chapter we will examine each component part of the proposal and the rationale for including it. We will detail the possible plans according to the type of research you wish to undertake.

Questions you will be able to answer after completing this chapter:

- How can I complete a project proposal that contains the required elements to provide for a reasonable project plan to be later developed?

- How can I demonstrate through my project proposal that I can write a successful research proposal outlining and evaluating the research process and method(s) most appropriate to investigate my research question/subject?

Having completed the sections and your courses on research methods, you should be familiar with the most popular potential methodologies and methods that you could be expected to use and what types of research they would most commonly be used for. In your proposal you will be expected to make an argument, clearly and directly, about which methodology and which method/s would be most suitable for your particular project and you should now be able to do this.

Key points that you should take away from this chapter are:

- one size does not fit all – there are as many possible project proposals as there are possible projects but different methods may be more appropriate for some topics than others;
- clarity in writing and discussion will enable a more successful project and successful supervision;
- realistic sizing of a project and timescales are essential to the completion of a successful project; and
- projects grounded in past literature are likely to have clear objectives and research questions.

Project proposals

A project requires a methodical approach; an unbiased attitude; a clear view of what is fact and what is reported as 'fact'; and the ability to take relevant information and data and turn them into a coherent and logical whole. The proposal demonstrates how you will ensure that the final project will undertake this. It demonstrates the significance of the research; its originality; and its contribution to knowledge and understanding.

A proposal should contain:

- Purpose of the project:
  - to understand the details;
  - to 'sell' an idea.

Parts/Contents of the report:

- Title;
- Table of contents;
- Synopsis (executive summary – abstract) summary which:
  - highlights research question and answers from the study;
  - recounts recommendations and implementation.
- Introduction:
  - broad problem or issue;
  - background and rationale for study;
  - literature review;
  - specifying problem statement;
  - identifying research questions;
  - theoretical framework and hypotheses;
  - nature and type of study;
  - time horizon;
  - study setting;
  - unit of analysis;
  - transition to next section on methodology.
- Methodology section:
  - research design issues;
  - population and sample;
  - variables;
  - measures;
  - data collection;
  - data analysis.
- Results section.
  - anticipated results.
- Recommendations anticipated and implementation issues assumed.
- References.
- Appendix: PERT chart.

Contents of a project proposal

Project proposals will vary widely according to the topic of interest, and other factors. For this reason, there is no set format that will always work. Experience has shown, however, that all good project proposals seem to have the following features in common.

They state the problem or issue that the project will cover – detailing its aims and objectives. Here you want to include information on why you chose your project, how it can help your further development as a manager or expert in your chosen field, and what you are trying to discover. You'll want a clear aim of what you intend to answer in the project. This is the problem definition. You will add one or two research questions if appropriate, but will certainly have two or more objectives that you intend the project to achieve.

In the box below are five examples of how some students have written their aims and objectives. Only two have merit. Which would you have liked to write? And why?

Examples of Aims and Objectives for Proposals

Example 1: I have decided to research this topic because I believe that organizations that engage in corporate social responsibility (CSR) help the society and community in which they operate. I believe that they also benefit the shareholders financially and I intend to discover by what amount they do so, in comparison to companies that do not undertake CSR. I will be basing my research on two organizations in Western Africa.

Example 2: Corporate social responsibility is high on the agenda of multinational organizations. How can organizations make profits and at the same time benefit the communities in which they operate? I will base my research on two comparative organizations in Western Africa.

Example 3: Maximizing retail densities, increasing product sales and driving category margins without damaging a brand's perception require in-depth inductive and deductive research and analysis (Keller, Aperia and Georgson, 2008).

Though not entirely in agreement with the famous statement by Roy Spence of the GSD&M Agency (Levine, 2006) that 'what you stand for as a brand is as important as what you sell, because everybody's selling the same thing', the UK high street has become one of the most competitive retail environments in Europe.

The primary objective of this research is to measure whether campaign imagery when used in store windows or in the in-store environment improves consumer sales of the particular product featured in the campaign imagery. Is there a direct product ROI?

Example 4: The Basel Committee on Banking Supervision responded to the crisis by adopting a series of reforms to strengthen resilience of banks. Here in the UK, the Independent Commission on Banking chaired by Sir John Vickers (Vickers Committee) made recommendations which aim to create more stable UK banking in the long term. Banks report 87% higher compliance costs. In this current economic climate, with the regulators' renewed affirmation towards compliance and bankers' defiance towards new regulations, I would be interested to find out if increased compliance costs will drive technology innovation and adoption within UK banks.

Example 5: Many of today's businesses operate in a continual state of crisis and have become burdened with non-essential and ineffective business processes. Business process modelling helps in identifying, describing and understanding current business processes and enables investigation of alternative business practices. This project involves a survey of some of the popular methods and tools used for business process modelling and their comparison using a case study in a pharmaceutical company.

Proposals identify the relevant literature (academic and 'civilian') that the project will draw upon. You'll need a few specific 'starting points' – articles, books and the like that will let a supervisor know if you are headed in the right direction. Review journals, key texts and articles as appropriate, and explain how these will inform the project aim. At this stage you will not be able to review the entire field, but must ensure that you review the most important theories for your project.

The purpose of a review is to analyse critically a segment of a published body of knowledge through summary, classification and comparison of prior research studies, reviews of literature and theoretical articles.

Examples of literature reviews are too long to be given here but you must ensure that what you review is as up to date as feasible. This is the initial literature that you are basing your research questions on and if it is too old, then your question might already have been answered.

Proposals detail the methodology that is to be used in the project. Note that the word here is methodology, not method. What this means is that you need to come up with a logical connection between the focus of your project and the ways in which you propose to conduct it. You'll want to *justify* your methodology. Remember that the methodology is the part of the work that tells the reader how you intend to come to an understanding of how you will know when you've found out what you want to know – when you have answered your research question and achieved your objectives:

- Have you decided upon a methodology?

- Have you chosen the methodology to help you proceed? This can be a consultancy methodology such as action research, or an academic methodology such as qualitative or quantitative.

- Can you justify the methodology you've chosen?

- Are you familiar with the basic requirements of the methodology?

Be sure that if there are multiple ways of conducting your project, you have provided coherent reasons as to why the choice you made is the best choice. This is the first stage of your research design.

When it comes to the precise methods you intend to use, don't simply make a bold statement like 'I'll use interviews.' Rather, say something more specific, like 'I'll interview 25 salespersons who work in the capital goods industry using a combination of structured and unstructured techniques.' You want to be as specific as you can in this section, and try to justify each choice you've made.

Remember: qualitative research is designed to answer the *who*, *how* and *why* questions in research. It aims for in-depth understanding of a phenomenon rather than a broad overview. It uses a variety of methods to describe and translate meaning from the data.

It relies on a subjective interpretation of the data – no two people may see the same things – and thus requires triangulation if at all possible or what is known as 'inter-rating' where another person with a similar background looks at the data and validates the researcher's choice of meaning. You will need to demonstrate understanding and interpretation. You may use smaller samples and there will be contextual involvement.

Quantitative research looks for a measurement – as precise as is feasible. Used for theory (also called hypotheses) building or testing. *How much? How often? How many? When? Who?* You will need to describe, explain and predict. You will need to demonstrate a distinction between fact and judgement. Consistency is crucial.

For every method that you detail, you must also detail the sample to be used and justify this sample. You must also specify the analysis method for every piece of data to be collected and again justify why this way of analysing is the best and most suitable.

Ensure that for quantitative studies you include the names of any statistical tests that you will utilize and why these are most suitable.

Examples of Method Justification

Example 1: I intend to interview both middle and senior management in my organization. I will use both semi-structured and unstructured interviews as appropriate. I will undertake a pilot of my interviews with a friend. The interviews will last between 20 and 30 minutes and I will video these interviews. I will interview 10 people in total and I will ensure that I can quote them.

Example 2: I will collect secondary data through journal papers and books. I will collect my primary data by interviewing some staff in charge of CSR but I will be flexible about what questions I ask. I will use theming to analyse my data.

Example 3: During this research process, I propose a mixed methods approach combining quantitative and qualitative research techniques to be able to get a rounded and complete picture. The researcher plans to collect secondary data from information available in the public domain. Additionally, the researcher proposes to collate primary data via a questionnaire and semi-structured interviews conducted on a sample population obtained through snowball sampling.

Example 4: This project proposes to undertake a combination of primary quantitative and qualitative research with deductive and inductive learning outcomes, using primary empirical data collected at POS, analysis of historical like-for-like sales data, correlations and causality experiments, field research in the form of consumer behaviour and naturalism, as well as focus group questionnaires and or interviews.

None of these is perfect. What could you have written? And what are these examples missing?

Project proposals detail the scope and limitations of the project. Here you want to suggest the boundaries of the systems that your project proposes to explore. Too wide an exploration of a topic will almost inevitably lead to failure. Too narrow an exploration of a topic will lead to triviality.

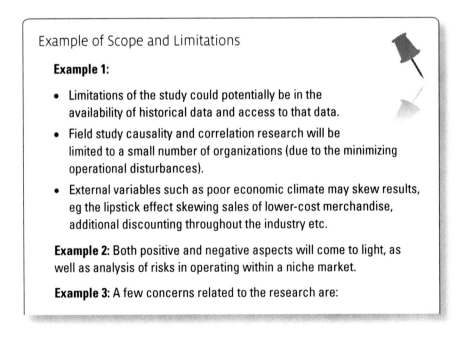

Example of Scope and Limitations

Example 1:

- Limitations of the study could potentially be in the availability of historical data and access to that data.
- Field study causality and correlation research will be limited to a small number of organizations (due to the minimizing operational disturbances).
- External variables such as poor economic climate may skew results, eg the lipstick effect skewing sales of lower-cost merchandise, additional discounting throughout the industry etc.

Example 2: Both positive and negative aspects will come to light, as well as analysis of risks in operating within a niche market.

Example 3: A few concerns related to the research are:

- No prior experience in carrying out a research project. Guidance would be a great asset from tutors and supervisors to ensure the research is a success.
- The quantitative part of the research may not get the required response from people.
- To ensure that my preconceived ideas within the field of marketing do not lead the research. Instead understand the requirements from the target community.

Examples of Resource Justifications

Example 1: The research project has a tight timescale as it is linked to a live project. A certain amount of time and resource needs to be dedicated to create mock-ups.

Example 2: Time will be a big factor as I have limited amounts of time to spend on this project as I have to work part-time.

Example 3: I need the money to fly out to conduct my interviews in West Africa and I assume that the university will assist me in this.

Projects identify the resources that the project will require. This includes time, and any money, eg for flights overseas if you need to go home to conduct interviews. It is all too common for students to 'bite off more than they can chew' with a project, and by thinking about this question in advance, it may help you to be clear what you are able to accomplish. If you do not have the money to fly home or overseas if your project is not set in this country, consider interviews by Skype, phone or e-mail.

Projects provide a timeline for project completion. If all has gone well in the project proposal so far, you should be able to provide a plan for action to complete the project.

If you are not familiar with PERT charts, see http://searchsystems-management.techtarget.com/sDefinition/0,,sid20_gci331391,00.html or http://web2.concordia.ca/Quality/tools/20pertchart.pdf for an overview of this technique as you might want to use this to help you plan.

Also, try identifying a few key stages (milestones) in the project (eg literature review completed, data collection starts, data collection finishes, first draft to supervisor etc) and set these out.

A key reason for difficulty in completing the project is the lack of a realistic timetable with achievable targets for completion. Don't spend too little time on this step – you'll suffer if you don't plan your time well. At the same time, don't spend too much time on drawing pretty PERT charts. Little is to be gained at this stage from overly detailed charts. But do ensure that you leave time at the end for proofreading, checking references and adding a correct contents list etc – this usually takes one to two weeks.

Projects provide an ethical statement. Universities now require students to consider the ethical implications of their research. Your research should not be conducted in such a way as to cause harm to any of its participants – or its researchers. Participation in the research should not cause mental or physical harm to anyone. Your research should be conducted honestly, accurately and as fully as possible so as not to mislead. You must not plagiarize or use the research or intellectual property of others and any work put into your project by others should be acknowledged.

It is likely that your university will have an Ethics Committee and will have drawn up an ethics form for you to fill in. Ensure that you complete this fully.

Critical and analytical thinking

It is important that when drawing up your proposal, you use critical analytical thinking. You must answer the following questions in your proposal:

1. What is the main line of your reasoning?

2. Is the line of reasoning clear in your introduction and conclusion?

3. What is the key evidence that you intend to collect to support your line of reasoning and achieve your objectives?

4. Have you provided the literature and research methodology and methods in such a way as to support your line of reasoning by demonstrating that they will collect the required evidence?

5. Can you ensure that the evidence you produce – including the literature – is up to date and how will you demonstrate that it is relevant?

6. Will you be able to provide enough evidence to support your line of reasoning? What might you miss and why will that not matter?

7. How will you analyse your evidence to support your line of reasoning?

8. Have you presented the proposal in such a way that it follows logically?

9. Could there be alternative ways to look at this evidence or to collect the data or interpret the data? If so, why will your way better support your line of reasoning?

If you have managed all the above then it is likely that you are well prepared to begin your project. Remember that the better prepared the proposal is then the better your project is likely to be.

Prior planning prevents poor performance

Hints About *Your* Project Plan

1. Do you have enough time to do the project?

2. Do you have, or can you get, all of the resources needed to undertake the project?

3. Have you got a clear idea of the main stages of the project, and can you assign each of them to a schedule?

4. Have you left time for working with your supervisor? (Remember their holidays!)

5. When will you send out the first survey/interviews?

6. Have you left enough time to do this twice if you need to do so?

7. Have you left enough time for interviewees to be sick, have holidays etc and thus not be available to your schedule?

8. Have you left time for writing up?

Remember you should be working concurrently, not consecutively.

04
Collecting quantitative data

Finding quantitative data

This chapter considers the type of quantitative data that you can obtain and the various methods by which you can collect them.

Questions you will be able to answer after completing this chapter:

- What type of quantitative data can I collect? And for what purpose?
- What will be the purpose of collecting these data?

The key point you should take away from this chapter is that the data that you will collect will come to you in a number of forms:

1. As a result of a survey – this is primary data.

2. As a result of looking at archival documents, in an organization for instance – depending on your methodology this may be considered primary data, but more typically will be considered secondary data.

3. As a result of looking at datasets on various websites etc – this is primary data when used for new calculations but secondary data when used as evidence and not used for any calculations.

In the sections below we will look at each type of data and how you can collect them.

Secondary data

Looking first at secondary datasets, there are significant numbers of these freely available to students depending on their prime discipline and research question.

In particular, the most common source will be ESDS – the Economic and Social Data Service – which contains a good source of data and databanks, both national and international, such as:

- large-scale government surveys;
- multinational databanks and surveys;
- longitudinal surveys;
- qualitative and mixed methods data; and
- research data management.

Remember that you can search data that have been deposited by other researchers, data that have been deposited by governments and their agencies and data that are collected by a number of organizations both here and abroad.

Look also at:

- market research companies;
- company websites, internal documents, press releases;
- the media and polling agencies;
- lobbyists;
- official government sites;
- international bodies such as the United Nations and the World Health Organization.

When using websites such as media and company sites you need to consider a number of points:

- *Relevance and validity.* The information and data should be of the right type for their purpose. These secondary data were not collected for your project and thus the data may be incomplete and may not contain some of the elements that you are researching. Thus how valid are they? And how reliable?

Are they trying to make a point? Think carefully about campaigning websites here.

- *Precision*. The data supplied need to be at the right level of precision for your project. You may need statistics to be at a certain level of percentage points of validity, eg 56.78 rather than 56.8 or even 57. It is normal for large numbers to be rounded up and this may not be useful to you. Would you rather know exactly how many people live in Greater London or the approximate number of 8 million? What level of precision will your project require?

- *Currency*. How up to date are the data? Was the figure of 8 million for Greater London calculated in 2007 or 2012? How important is it for you to know this level of currency? Is the figure up to date enough for you to use for forecasting – if this is required in your project?

- *Completeness*. Are all the necessary data there? Have they missed off one London council because it was difficult to obtain the population statistics – or have they just estimated this figure? Remember, when looking at websites that are being used to showcase organizations or software programs or some other particular viewpoint, that while they may not lie, they may miss data and information that do not suit their purpose. Thus drug manufacturers will quote the six studies that say that their drug is safe, and miss the one that says it isn't.

- *Clarity*. Can you actually work out what the data are and extract them without wading through unnecessary waffle and bumf?

- *Authority*. Who has authored the web page or information that you are intending to use? Have they been clearly identified as the author of the work? And are they suitable authors? Remember that consultants are not academics and you must assume that all White Papers produced by such consultancies, unless paid for as research for a recognized authority, will be intending to show the consultancy's skills off, and the organization in a good light. They may well be very useful in terms of understanding what practitioners are thinking and doing, but they are usually not underpinned by academic rigour.

- *Verification.* Can you verify that the data are accurate? The author is accurate? The organization is clearly spelled out? And so on. That is, can you check that the information being supplied is being supplied by a bona fide organization?

Taking as an example the following research question: What is the requirement for social housing in Manchester?

Exercise

Write down three to five databases you would like to use to find data to answer the question.

Link each database to one of the following objectives of the research:

1. To enable Manchester City Council to build sufficient social housing for the next 30 years.

2. To ensure that the social housing built is fit for purpose and population.

Did your answer look something like this?

TABLE 4.1 Answer to social housing exercise

Objective	Databases
To enable Manchester City Council to build sufficient social housing* for the next 30 years.	Population statistics; immigration and migration; current lists of houses; waiting lists.
To ensure that the social housing built is fit for purpose and population.	Demographics, eg age, disabilities, family size, and so on.

* Social housing is housing built for people who cannot afford normal levels of rent, perhaps because they are disabled or are out of work etc. People will be on a waiting list for these houses/flats and will be allocated appropriate housing according to a points system based on perceived need.

Now look at ESDS to see exactly what databases would be available for you to look at containing the data you would need to work with.

What you are looking for is details of what Manchester's current need for social housing is; what housing stock they have already; who is in this housing; population movements for the city; and projections for the future relating to all of the above.

And thus what social housing needs to be built – ie what the gap is between what is currently provided and what should be provided, and when it should be provided. As the UK's population ages we are likely to need fewer larger houses and more flats or small houses.

The second part of the research is to ensure that the housing built is fit for purpose. That is to say, that there will be enough housing for children in suitable areas, ie near schools and playgroups, GPs and so on; that there will enough sheltered housing for the infirm and so on.

How well did you do?

You might wish to have a discussion relating to politics here as the current government (2013) has indicated that social housing cannot be expected to be for 'life'. That is, if you are in a four-bedroomed home and there are now only two of you, you may be required to move to something smaller; and also that if you can now afford commercial rents as your circumstances have changed, then you may be required to give up your social housing. Take care here not to be biased but merely to point out the implication of such a programme on the provision of social housing – relate it to the demographics perhaps – as our population is growing older in general, will this mean that we will need more smaller houses/flats to accommodate those who are made to move under this programme, and will this mean fewer larger houses will need to be built as they will be vacated through this?

Having identified where the data are, you need to now retrieve them in a form that is suitable for your analysis. In your research design for utilizing secondary datasets, you will have identified the most suitable techniques for turning these data into a format that fulfils your objectives. Typically these will be statistical techniques. See the section on 'Analysing quantitative data'.

If you are not sure how to use these techniques (within SPSS or other suitable software) then you need to consult a specialist book to learn how to do this – see the references section – or use the websites indicated.

Primary data

The most common way of undertaking primary quantitative data collection is through a survey. Here you will be collecting primary data for analysis.

Many students immediately think of undertaking a survey when they attempt to obtain their data. The reality is that undertaking a survey not only requires extensive pre-work to justify each question, but also requires a significant number of responses to be valid. A lot of people are 'surveyed out' and attempting to obtain sufficient numbers of responses is becoming tricky. Most universities suggest that a minimum of 50–70 participants is required for validity of a survey research study.

You must ensure:

- That each question has an analysis method related to it and that in combination these analyses provide answers to the research question and achieve the objectives.

- That the questions are linked to hypotheses that are derived from academic theory and obtained from the literature. If you use a questionnaire that you have obtained from literature, a website or a book, working back to the theory can be difficult, unless that is provided to you. Beware of plagiarism at this point! Using other people's links back to academic theory implies that they have undertaken the literature research in order to find these theories. It is then tricky to integrate their literature and theory into your analysis. Unless this is a seminal survey, and thus it is theoretically important that you use a pre-prepared questionnaire, it is better to create your own.

Designing a successful survey

This section looks at how to design a successful survey. A survey collects numerical data that then can be analysed through statistics. In this section we will not look at the statistical techniques for analysis but the ways that these data can be collected. There are a number of survey methods and we will consider which type of data collection method is the most appropriate for the particular research being conducted.

Questions you will be able to answer after completing this section:

- Which method of data collection through a survey would be the most suitable in varying situations?
- What are the pros and cons of each data collection method?
- What is a suitable sample for data collection? And which methods should I use to achieve this sample?

Key points that you should take away from this section are:

- When conducting a survey, not all the data collected will necessarily be numerical, and it is possible also to collect textual data that can then be analysed through, say, content analysis. These types of data, in addition to the numerical, can lead to very rich data.
- Surveys can be conducted in differing ways and it is essential to ensure that you are using the most appropriate for the type of research you are undertaking. It should be noted that obtaining a sample that is statistically significant when undertaking a survey that is external to an organization is very difficult, and thus ways to alleviate this issue need to be considered.

Surveys are designed around hypotheses and it is important to ensure that you have sufficient questions to test these hypotheses and thus questions may need to be phrased in different ways to test important hypotheses – both positively and negatively.

Example of literature from which a hypothesis is derived

The dominant role of strategy in knowledge management had been known to researchers and practitioners alike for many years as they knew that the selection of strategy by a company will determine whether it places its importance on humans or systems (Choi and Lee,

2002); how it is going to serve its clients; hire its employees; and employ the economies of its business (Hansen, Nohria and Tierney, 1999). In fact, according to earlier research, the whole of the management of KM depends on the strategy it selects. Firms select their KM strategies to match their culture, capabilities and priorities (Wiig, 1997), and the most appropriate strategy is the one that meets its highly contextual needs (Wong, 2005).

Hypothesis that is developed from the literature:

H1: Organizations that have a well-understood knowledge management (KM) strategy successfully develop a system for capturing knowledge from their experience.

TABLE 4.2 Example of how hypotheses should link to questions

	Hypothesis	Survey question(s) used
H1:	Organizations that have a well-understood knowledge management (KM) strategy successfully develop a system for capturing knowledge from their experience.	Our knowledge is clearly structured, making it easy to add to and draw from it. In my organization the knowledge management programme has resulted in people working together in communities of practice. We did not normally work in teams, but the introduction of the knowledge management programme has resulted in people working together in teams.
H2:	Organizations that have a well-understood KM strategy utilize intranet for exchanging ideas, information and knowledge.	Our intranet is the primary channel of internal communication for exchanging ideas, information and knowledge.

| H3: | Organizations that have a well-understood KM strategy develop a specific technology for managing the collective knowledge of the organization. | My organization does not employ any specific technology for the purpose of managing collective knowledge. |
| | | My organization uses a knowledge management programme to share knowledge. |

Methods of collecting survey data

Method 1: Phone surveys

Can your expected participant clearly articulate their attitude, motivation, intention or expectation? Can you phrase your questions clearly enough that they can do this?

If so, and if you can persuade sufficient numbers to participate, then you can go ahead.

Method 2: Self-administered surveys

As with phone surveys, can your participants understand the questions clearly enough and express themselves? And can you persuade sufficient numbers to participate? Self-administered surveys are often supplied on paper or through websites.

Method 3: Mail surveys

These are now not very common, but are low cost, work well when targeted precisely; but often have very low response rates, and require significant time for development to ensure that they are easy and quick to answer.

Method 4: Interview surveys

You conduct these in person but there is no deviation from the questions set. These may use a computer to store the results. They have the advantage of a good completion rate but they are time-consuming – remember you need as many completed surveys as through any other method. You will frequently see marketing people standing on shop frontages to try and get these completed. They do have the advantage that you can ensure you obtain the correct demographics for your survey as you persuade people to complete them, but they need to be short and quick to complete. They will also miss sensitive or complex issues and don't permit people to express opinions that are not catered for on the questionnaire. They have an advantage, however, in that the person undertaking the work doesn't need necessarily to be the researcher, as no knowledge of the reason behind the questions is required to administer the survey.

Method 5: Web-based surveys

These are increasingly common through such online sites as Survey-Monkey. They have made many of the issues relating to survey a thing of the past as the cost of administering such a survey is very low – they are often free for students provided you do not require a very high response rate – and they can attract through links in the social media participants who otherwise would not participate. E-mail links, for instance, can be programmed, as can website links. Unfortunately, you cannot ensure the demographics of your sample or your response rate or even that those who go to the site actually answer truthfully – always an issue, of course, with any research but surveys are particularly prone to this problem. The survey does need to be attractive and easy and quick to answer.

Advantages include the fact that participants feel anonymous especially as the surveys may attract large numbers; you can attract participants from across many countries (a knowledge management survey conducted by one of the authors of this book attracted participants from over 70 countries); you can analyse the data at many different points of time (we downloaded the data at regular intervals), which allows trends to be analysed; and you can obtain very quick results (one survey we set up obtained over 70 responses in less than a week). Additionally, these surveys can be multilingual and are very easy to import into Excel or SPSS or to design your own reports.

Designing your questionnaire

The first step is to lay out the objective of the investigation. This should be as specific, clear-cut and unambiguous as possible.

Consider whether you are looking for opinions and attitudes or factual characteristics or behaviours – or a combination of the two.

Planning is the one of the most critical stages in a survey as you do not have the opportunity to go back to your participants and ask further questions if you got it wrong the first time or missed important questions out. You need to be very sure that your questions are phrased in such a way that you get the answer in the format that you want. Mistakes are easily made at this stage.

Look at the following statement. Can you phrase this differently and get a different answer?

Do you favour cutting programmes such as social security, Medicare, Medicaid and farm subsidies to reduce the public deficit?
Answers: 23% agree; 65% oppose; 11% no opinion.

What if you asked this question?

Do you favour cutting government entitlements to reduce the public deficit?

Would the answer be the same?

In fact, exactly this set of questions was asked in the *Wall Street Journal* and the response was 61 per cent in favour; 25 per cent oppose; and 14 per cent no opinion for the second question.

Note also that these are questions that can be answered yes/no/no opinion. Normally when we ask survey questions we will use a scale that permits more refinement in answers – this is called the Likert scale. Likert scales usually offer a participant five or seven possible answers, either numerically or in text form. You will decide how many potential answers you might want to your questions depending on: a) how many layers of possibilities you want to offer; and b) how and with which software package you intend to analyse your answers. Usually the more refinement you offer, the more sophisticated the package you will need to use to analyse.

Determinants of response rate are many but will include the following:

- *The length of your questionnaire.* Normally the longer it is the fewer people will answer and the more they will skip. So try to make your questionnaire look small – if you are using a paper-based survey, then utilize the column format and margins in your document to put as many questions onto one side of paper as are reasonable and can still be seen! You should also double-side. If you are using a web-based survey then indicate at the beginning how long you expect the completion of the survey to take. Try and underestimate slightly to encourage people... you can also use the facility which shows how much of the survey has been completed when using web surveys.

- *Privacy.* What type of questions are you asking? And how much do they invade people's privacy? Will people be willing to divulge certain items to you? And consider the ethics of what you asking too – and whether your questions will need ethical approval. The more personal the questions, the less likely people are to answer.

- *Attitudes towards the research topic.* Are people interested in this topic? Would they like to receive a short report of the responses you received? Is it about a topic that is current and broad enough to gain a good response or is it about something very narrow that will interest very few people? The more relevance the topic has to people, the more they are likely to answer.

- *The amount of free time people are likely to have to answer –* eg a student may have more time than a CEO!

- *How much the survey is personalized –* eg does it accompany a personal e-mail etc?

The more sensitive a topic is, the less likely people are to answer these questions in an anonymous survey.

Things to note:

- There is a direct relationship between the questionnaire length, question complexity and question sensitivity and the mode of collection of these data.

- There can be a measurement problem when people are asked to report past events. People will tend to under-report the less prominent items – a memory issue?

- Be very careful to ask questions that can be answered with a yes/no or are closed when you are not asking for explanations.

- If at all possible, complement the closed questions with a small number of open questions to ask for your participant's opinion. This is helpful for two reasons: first, they like to be asked what they think; and second, they may come up with some ideas that you had not thought of.

- Be very careful not to ask leading questions – phrasing is all-important.

Data analysis plan

- Every question asked in a survey must link to a hypothesis and must also link to expected methods of analysis. Every data objective must be represented in the survey.

- It is also likely that you will need a demographics section to 'set' your data in their background. This may include gender; age; role; company background etc depending on the topic matter. It is important to monitor this demographics section to ensure that you end up with a suitable mix according to your topic – eg enough of all ages; enough of all industry sectors, so that you can target more responses of the correct type if needed.

References

Brace, I (2004) *Questionnaire Design*, Kogan Page, London

Choi, B and Lee, H (2002) Knowledge management strategy and its link to knowledge creation process, *Expert Systems with Applications*, 23(3), pp 173–87

Fowler, Jr FJ (2009) *Survey Research Methods*, 4th edn, Sage, London

Hansen, MT, Nohria, N and Tierney, T (1999) What's your strategy for managing knowledge? *Harvard Business Review*, 77(2), pp 106–16

Lavrakas, PJ (2008) *Encyclopedia of Survey Research Methods*, Sage, London

Sapsford, R (2007) *Survey Research*, 2nd edn, Sage, London

Schonlau M (2009) Selection bias in web surveys and the use of propensity scores, *Sociological Methods & Research*, 37(3), 291–318

Wiig, KM (1997) Integrating intellectual capital and knowledge management, *Long Range Planning*, 30(3), pp 399–405

Wong, KY (2005) Critical success factors for implementing knowledge management in small and medium enterprises, *Industrial Management and Data Systems*, 105(3), pp 261–79

YouTube (2011) UIC Survey Research Methods Online Certificate Program: four webinars www.youtube.com/watch?v=tRUBscxcSTs

YouTube (2010) Neill, J, Lecture 1 – Introduction to Survey Research Parts 1–4 www.youtube.com/watch?v=rjO3t6uVXuQ www.youtube.com/watch?v=NVDnsWeODGM

05
Collecting qualitative data through interviews

T he purpose of this chapter is to focus on types of interviews as qualitative methods of data collection. It discusses how primary data can be collected using semi-structured, in-depth and group interviews, also known as focus groups. The appropriateness of using these interviews in relation to different research strategies is also discussed. Advice on how to undertake such interviews is given, including the conduct of focus groups; internet-mediated (including online); and telephone interviews. Note that developing a research design may incorporate more than one type of interview.

Questions you will be able to answer after completing this chapter:

- How can I classify research interviews and understand the purpose of each type?

- Which research situations favour the use of group, semi-structured and in-depth interviews? And what are their limitations?

- How can I develop my competence to undertake group, semi-structured and in-depth interviews? And will I understand the logistical and resource issues that affect their use?

- What are the advantages and disadvantages of using one-to-one and group interviews including focus groups, in particular contexts?

- What are the issues and advantages of conducting interviews by telephone and via the internet or intranet?

Key points that you should take away from this chapter are:

- Qualitative interviewing is a research tool that allows the collection of a rich and detailed set of data; however, you need to develop a sufficient level of competence to conduct these types of interview, and you also need to secure access to the type of data associated with their use.

- It is recommended that you practise interviewing and ensure that your supervisor has checked over your questions before you set out for your first one. Remember that you only get one shot at any interview. So if you forget a question you will not be able to go back for the answer later.

- In-depth and semi-structured interviews can be used with quantitative research to become what is called mixed methods research. The nature of the research strategy, along with the other issues related to the significance of establishing personal contact and the length of time required from those who provide data will determine which type of interviews to use.

- Data quality issues and logistical and resource matters will need to be considered when using in-depth and semi-structured interviews.

- Apart from one-to-one interviews conducted on a face-to-face basis, interviews may be conducted by telephone or electronically in particular circumstances. In addition, group interviews such as focus groups may be used. There may be particular advantages associated with group interviews, but these are considerably more difficult to manage than one-to-one interviews. Note that there are software programs that can assist in transcribing digital recordings of interviews. Consider the format in which you will interview.

- You must ensure that you sample correctly when setting up your interviews – see the section on data saturation (page 149).

When setting up interviews you will usually have to go through someone who is called – in research terms – a 'gatekeeper'.

This is the person who gives permission and will make the contacts for you. If you can arrange for them to give you an interview schedule it will be easier for you, but it is not always possible.

There may be 'bars' in interviewing that you will need to consider:

- The interviewee may have an ulterior motive in what they are reporting and how they are reporting it – office politics for instance.

- The informant may wish to please you – the interviewer – so that their opinions may be well received.

- Be aware of the surroundings so that distractions do not affect the interview itself – don't try interviewing in a café, for instance (as not only might the interviewee be distracted by the coffee and cakes, but the sounds of cups and clinking plates and other people's voices will make your recording difficult to transcribe), or somewhere where the interviewee may be distracted by e-mail bleeps or telephone calls.

- The interviewee may see you as being too young and therefore lack confidence in you – sufficiently as to not answer in depth or in full.

- Be careful if your interviewee asks to see a full set of questions in advance – they may then have the set of 'prepared' answers given to them perhaps by superiors.

- Ensure that the interviewee has sufficient time for the interview.

You will probably only manage two or at most three interviews a day, even assuming that you have little travel between each one, so ensure that this is planned well in advance.

After each interview read through your notes and before you transcribe them think and reflect about what you have learnt and make notes on how the interview went and the main points that you think you have learnt. Also reflect on how the interviewee looked – were they nervous? Were they hesitant in answering any questions? Did they look uncomfortable with any topic as it arose? These may be indicators where you touched a nerve or they weren't quite prepared for this line of questioning. Is it therefore something personal to them or something that should be further explored with other interviewees?

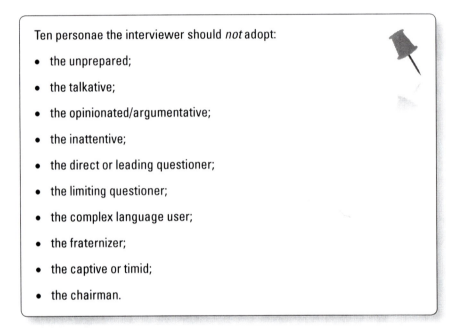

Ten personae the interviewer should *not* adopt:

- the unprepared;
- the talkative;
- the opinionated/argumentative;
- the inattentive;
- the direct or leading questioner;
- the limiting questioner;
- the complex language user;
- the fraternizer;
- the captive or timid;
- the chairman.

Transcribing of notes should be done as soon as possible after the interview in case the recording is not complete or 'fuzzy' in parts, then your memory can help you fill in the blanks – as can the notes you took after the interview. You can transcribe into Word or straight onto an analysis program. It's your choice.

Type two copies of this transcription. Keep one copy locked so it cannot be edited, and then you will always have an original. The second copy can then be manipulated with other interviews as you start analysing meaning.

Interviewing types and design

There are two main types of interview with variations between the extremes:

1. Unstructured to surface (often preliminary) issues, using broad, open-ended questions, and obtaining indications of the perceptions of individuals.

2. Structured (semi) with a predetermined list of questions – if there are no unstructured questions then it is a quantitative interview.

It is always important to note that interviews can touch on very personal issues for the interviewee and thus you will need to be very aware of your participant's reaction to any question that you ask. You are exploring their real-life situation.

A good interview will focus on the subject's world and talk in their own 'language'. Interviewees will then respond on their own terms and in their own words.

Unstructured interviews

These are a type of conversation that is developed through a sustained time between the participant and the interviewer. Researchers need to listen intently and permit their interview participants to speak freely and without interruption.

In this type of interview there will be few, if any, pre-formulated questions and, in principle, no time limit, but you may need a set of prompts for yourself – or an aide-memoire – to ensure that you cover all the points you intended. The interviewee will develop their own frame of reference and to some extent this will become part of their life story. They will tend to use their own language and acronyms and you can interrupt – if you only do this occasionally – to ask what these mean. It might be better, though, to try and explore this area at the beginning before you begin the long interview.

Semi-structured interviews

These types of interview ensure that some consistency is maintained between interviews, as a number of pre-formulated open questions are asked, usually in a set order.

Questioning techniques

When structuring an interview you need to consider what type of questions to ask and how to ask them. It is suggested that you:

- start by introducing yourself and the purpose of the interview;
- funnel questions – moving from broad themes to narrower; use 'warm-up' easy-to-answer questions;
- try to use unbiased questions: you must not 'lead' the answer or the interviewee;
- try to clarify any issues that arise in your mind by asking supplementary questions – but don't get involved in the discussion yourself, just listen;
- try to help the respondent to think through issues – but don't make affirmative noises such as 'Good' or distressed noises such as 'Oh dear';
- use mirroring language – ie the same types of phrases as your interviewee;
- be flexible if they bring up things you hadn't thought of but that seem interesting and relevant;
- be aware of any sensitive topics you wish to discuss and make sure they are comfortable in discussing them;
- ensure that you questions are open-ended and don't require a simple yes/no answer;
- don't make assumptions about what the interviewee knows – check that they understand fully;
- avoid 'leading' questions;
- try to look interested at all times – keep good eye contact and don't slouch;
- ensure that you ask some 'cooling-off' questions at the end – very straightforward – and then remember to thank the interviewee (and say goodbye); and
- take as detailed notes as you can – you must be careful with taping – only if permitted and remember that technology can go wrong so don't rely on a tape only.

A semi-structured interview has a guide attached to it, which is used for all interviews. Here the topics will be specified in advance and the sequence of questions and wording of questions are carefully worked out.

This is done for good analytical reasons:

1. It means that it is much easier to compare interviews as you can look answer by answer.

2. It ensures that the questions are comprehensive.

3. And that there are no logical gaps.

However, there are also downsides to working from a guide for the inexperienced interviewer:

1. Important topics can be missed.

2. Questions may need to be changed in order that interviewees understand – see mirroring of language. The answers may therefore also change and not match.

There are a number of YouTube links that can help you with interviewing. Try to work through them in the order listed:

Interviewing [by Graham Gibbs]: how to undertake a research interview: www.youtube.com/watch?v=FGH2tYuXf0s&feature=relmfu

Part 1: Interviews and the interview society: www.youtube.com/watch?v=9yRgBS2JmXU&feature=watch-vrec

Part 2: The pros and cons of interviewing: www.youtube.com/watch?v=4PbB2sAq-PQ&feature=watch-vrec

Part 3: Types of interview: www.youtube.com/watch?v=SWCh1RhYT-g&feature=watch-vrec

Part 4: The interview schedule: www.youtube.com/watch?v=8zFujnMFVtY&feature=relmfu

Part 5: The sequence of events and types of questions: www.youtube.com/watch?v=3hCPSE1Parg&feature=watch-vrec

Part 6: Good practice and technology: www.youtube.com/watch?v=dbaPz-7uCQk&feature=watch-vrec

Technology

When considering technology you need to think about the possibilities that it can offer you, especially if your interviewees are not co-located with either you or each other.

For instance:

- you can interview using Skype – with or without video recording;

- you can interview by e-mail, but this will not give the richness of face-to-face interviewing and permits the interviewee to consider carefully and perhaps to amend their answers; or

- you can interview by telephone – again this is not ideal as you cannot see a person's body language and words can be misunderstood etc.

Focus groups

Focus groups are an extension of interviewing but undertaken in a group. It can be thought of as eavesdropping on a conversation and as such can produce some very rich results.

It can be used on its own as the single research method or in combination with other methods, perhaps as an initial exploration of themes or issues that can be explored in one-to-one interviews. It is frequently used in market research and political research. It can obtain contextual background; generate hypotheses or propositions; elicit factors around a specific topic; field test a measuring instrument; and assist in the interpretation of the findings of previous research.

The topic that is explored needs to be easy to explain and not multifaceted where you are looking for some understanding.

Advantages:

1. It is highly efficient.

2. It weeds out extreme views and identifies where convergence lies.

3. No convergences are required but it allows participants to address issues that concern them.

4. Group dynamics stimulate people to think beyond their private ideas and help to formulate opinions and explanations.

5. It provides a forum for discussion, argument, probing and challenging viewpoints and their underlying reasons in a safe environment.

Planning required:

1. You will need to plan the role of the interviewee or facilitator so that they can guide, re-focus, and bring up salient issues during the session. This may need training or certainly practice.

2. It is useful to have a second person in the session in order that they can take notes and look after any recording devices being used. They can ensure that if videoing is taking place the camera is pointed at the person speaking or that tapes don't run out, or devices fail in any way etc. The facilitator/interviewee is too busy to undertake all of this as well.

3. The group should be as homogeneous as possible. Consider demographic and stratifying factors when considering participants. It is not a good idea, for instance, to include managers with staff as hierarchical issues may interfere with free speech – can you contradict a superior? Justify your samples (see section on sampling and research design).

4. You should have 7–12 participants in each group.

5. The session should last 45–60 minutes.

6. A guide of five to seven questions is required to steer the discussion in advance.

7. There is a discussion around how many focus groups you need to undertake. Some theorists recommend three or four groups but this will depend on the research question and how many relevant participants there might be. Certainly it is difficult to justify one group unless this group is carefully sampled.

Limitations of Focus Groups

Group effects:

- You may find that there are dominant participants where one person dominates the discussion and attempts to coerce all the group to their viewpoint.

- Or there may be the opposite where one person is reticent and never gives their viewpoint due to concern over social process or shyness.

- Or where dominance occurs there may be a group norm emerging whereby minority views are suppressed.

- Or the situation induces an uncritical thought process as everyone just complies with the norm.

Difficulty of setting up:

- Time intensive.

- Limits numbers of questions that can be considered due to time factors.

- Finding enough participants available at the same time.

- Lack of 'bribes' to entice participants – note you may wish to offer coffee and biscuits but nothing more should be offered. You should NOT start offering iPads or other 'prizes' for attendance – this is unethical for students.

Difficulty of analysing data:

- You will need to analyse not only verbal data but also body language.

- You may need to consider a variety of methods to analyse the data and this will be time-consuming and require you to become expert at using multiple techniques.

Example of a focus group using Monster Energy Drink

www.youtube.com/watch?v=eUU69-qbFZw&feature=related

Consider the above photo/video. Is this an appropriate place for a focus group to be held? Where would you hold a focus group in this situation? What facilities do you need to put in place? How do you invite participants? When do you invite participants?

Some people try to interview more than one person at the same time but not through setting up a focus group. This is not really a good idea as it is not controlled as there is no second person there, and it can be very difficult to ensure that everyone has the opportunity to speak.

An example of a focus group protocol is to be found in Remenyi (2011) p 81, plus other potentially useful examples of documents.

Other examples to be found online are:

Australian Civil-Military Centre: www.flickr.com/photos/civmil-coe/6958763792/ www.youtube.com/watch?v=CHj8EAmDM M8&feature=related

An online focus group as per the Observer: www.youtube.com/watch?v=5Z6xYd7NZFk&feature=watch-vrec

Interviewing references and further websites

Note that these are all Sage Publications books. Further details can be found on the Sage Publications website for journal articles, discussions and short talks.

Barbour R (2007) *Doing Focus Groups*

Chrzanowska, J (2002) *Interviewing Groups and Individuals in Qualitative Market Research*

Given, LM (2008) *The SAGE Encyclopedia of Qualitative Research Methods*

Holstein JA and Gubrium, JF (2003) *Inside Interviewing*

James N and Busher, H (2009) *Online Interviewing*

Krueger R, Casey, A (2009) *Focus Groups*

Kvale, S (2007) *Doing Interviews*

Lewis-Beck, MS, Bryman A, and Futing Liao, T (2004) *The SAGE Encyclopedia of Social Science Research Methods*

McCracken, G (1988) *The Long Interview*

Wengraf, T (2001) *Qualitative Research Interviewing*

Also see these websites:

http://online.sagepub.com/
www.edu.plymouth.ac.uk/resined/interviews/inthome.htm
www.ehow.com/way_5234507_qualitative-interviewing-
techniques.html
www.socialresearchmethods.net/kb/intrview.php
www.hse.gov.uk/stress/standards/pdfs/focusgroups.pdf

Chapter appendix: Interview Protocol
(adapted from Remenyi, 2011, p 39)

Item	Detail	Notes
Informant	Name	Position etc in organization etc
Location	Where interview to be held	Any particular things needed to bring or to organize for this location including map; ensure you leave enough time to arrive early to set up, cool down, go to the toilet etc.
Gatekeeper	Person who organized interview	Ensure they are thanked.
Organization	Product/services	Ensure you know and have read the website and any company reports and relevant newspapers for recent events that may impact on their answers or your questions.

Item	Detail	Notes
Setting up interview	Get recording set up. Explain the purpose. Name the gatekeeper and thank the interviewee for their time as well.	Make sure you have a letter of permission/consent for them to sign; include any confidentiality they want.
Interview schedule	If they request a copy of the questions, supply it.	Undertake the interview, ensuring that you cover all the points on your schedule and adding in any other that the interviewee deems appropriate. Thank them and shake hands if possible.
Note writing	Write the sets of notes as described in the section above.	Ensure that you write a reflective note as soon as possible after the interview.
		Don't forget to thank the gatekeeper formally after the interviews have been completed and remind them to thank again the interviewees.

NOTE   If you would like examples of a letter of introduction or informed consent then please see Remenyi (2011), pp 42–3.

Remenyi, D (2011) *Field Methods for Academic Research*, 2nd edition, Academic Publishing International, Reading

06
Collecting data as an ethnographer

There are a number of different ways that collecting data as an ethnographer can be undertaken by a student for their project. However, true ethnography cannot be undertaken as the student will not have time, unless they begin their project at the time they begin their studies and most students will not be that organized.

Saying that, one of my students suggested a way in which they could be a true ethnographer. He said:

> I am interested in ethnography, in particular the behaviour of my fellow students. I would like to study how they work in groups within class and within their assignment groups. I will keep a diary of my own experiences and analyse the behaviours I see around me. I can look at leadership and knowledge sharing and teamwork behaviours and can make some suggestions about how to improve such activities.

The issue, of course, is how ethical this study would be. Should he tell his fellow students what he is doing? And if he does, will their behaviour change as a result as per the Hawthorne effect? The Hawthorne effect is where subjects of the ethnographic study improve or modify an aspect of their behaviour that is being experimentally measured simply in response to the fact that they know that they are being studied. It is based on what happened when a researcher was looking at how people worked at the Hawthorne factory just outside

Chicago in the United States. The researcher found that as he measured output it changed and became slower if he was measuring for daily output against bonus payments for work above the anticipated average. Workers changed their speed of working to improve their chances of acquiring a bonus (see Gillespie, 1991).

If my student doesn't tell his fellow students and they find out later, what might their reaction be? And can he submit his observations of their behaviour without their knowledge?

Participant observation

Now is what is being suggested true ethnography or is it participant observation? Is it insider research? And what is the difference?

The definition of ethnography is: a qualitative research design aimed at exploring cultural phenomena (Hoey, 2013):

- It should be reflective – that is, you should keep a reflective diary about your observations.

- It should make a substantial contribution towards the understanding of the social life of humans – all projects should contribute to knowledge in some way, but here we are specifically looking at how humans interact.

- It should have an aesthetic impact on the reader – or at least some impact emotionally – it must affect the reader in some way.

- It should express a credible reality – the reader must believe the story and the report.

It should observe the world (the study) from the point of view of the subject (not the participant ethnographer).

The difference (in my view) is simple – it is ethnography if it lasts a long time, eg a year or six to nine months of immersion in the culture; it is participant observation if it takes less time and less emphasis is placed on some of the required outputs.

You can be a participant observer for just a week – say in an office where you undertake the work you are investigating as part of a larger study, eg the issues with the interface of a software system. You can become one of the users of the system and note for yourself the issues that arise when you try and undertake the work that the system was designed for.

This part of fieldwork helps you find out things that may not be mentioned in an interview:

- They may be forgotten or not realized as being important.

- It helps you find out some 'hidden' issues.

- You are able to look at the situation in the light of your own personal and theoretical knowledge and thus apply and link the theory to the practical work as you undertake it.

- It allows for reflection and introspection as a reflective diary would need to be kept.

Non-participative observation

It is also possible to observe and not participate in a situation. For instance, you could sit in the corner of an office and video the daily occurrences. The first day or two the occupants of that office will be acting outside their normal behaviour. After a while, though, they will forget you are there, provided you do not draw notice to yourself, and normal behaviour will resume.

Keep notes and ensure that you record conversations as well as video. And that you are able to record all happenings – you may need more than one camera or to choose your position very carefully so that you are not easily seen but can see easily.

Afterwards you will be able to analyse both voice patterns and body behaviour as well as actual activities. You will be able to see communication patterns and issues as they arise and how they are resolved – see the section on analysing qualitative data (pages 173–186).

This gives you an outsider's view rather than an insider's view.

Be careful about the concept of covert observations as this may be seen as 'Big Brother watching'. It is better to gain full permissions before you begin such observations.

References

Gillespie, R (1991) *Manufacturing knowledge: a history of the Hawthorne experiments*, Cambridge University Press, Cambridge

Hoey, B (2013) www.brianhoey.com/General%20Site/general_defn-ethnography.htm, accessed February 2013

Richardson, L (2000) Evaluating ethnography, *Qualitative Inquiry*, 6(2), 253–55

07
Case study research

Where students choose to research one or more corporate cases, how might cases be developed and reported effectively for a business project?

This chapter considers:

- The aims a) of researching a case, chiefly in studying the phenomenon that is contained in the student's research question; and b) of presenting it in the student's research report.

- The limits of usefulness for corporate cases and alternative ways that researchers use to present case findings, such as by drawing up space-saving tables that focus on core themes and elements of processes without articulating the entire processes.

- A case study is a research design that entails the detailed and intensive analysis of a single case. The term is sometimes extended to include the study of several cases for comparative purposes. It is an empirical enquiry that investigates a contemporary phenomenon in its real-life context and one that benefits from prior propositions based on the literature review and frequently is conducted through multiple data collection methods.

- We will discuss how to select a good case study – what are the key attributes that make a good case to study and what are the issues that might make studying that case difficult?

A case study is a slice of life. A project is a slice of living.

Objectives

After completing this chapter, you should be able to:

- demonstrate the reason as to why a particular case is viable for research;

- argue and justify the rationale for choosing a particular case or cases and propose the expected learnings from the case research that can be transferred to other research; and

- justify the various data collection methods you have chosen for your case study – selecting from interviews, ethnographic studies and documentation.

Key points that you should take away from this chapter are:

- That it is feasible to use just one case study for research but that there are a number of attributes that are required from this case to make it suitable. These attributes will depend on whether the case is intended to be exploratory, explanatory, descriptive, or illustrative where the research illustrates innovative practices.

- The analysis of case material is conducted through the various textual and qualitative tools but a small survey conducted within a case organization is also feasible.

- Case research aims to explore the phenomena under a particular context and does not commence with a notion about the limitations for the research.

- Your case comes with a historical background and a future and an existing interaction with the world outside it. All these may need to be considered to fully understand the phenomena under study.

CASE STUDY Exercise 1 (can be done in groups)

The company relations officer at your university offers you an internship at IKEA.

The intern will work with the group that is establishing new stores within China.

You have agreed to take this job and are going to use it as a case study for your project.

Activities:

- How would you start to design the case study research about entry strategies for the new Chinese stores?

- What sampling strategy would you develop to ensure that you talk to everyone concerned?

- How do you justify this sample?

- How will you know when you have reached data saturation?

- What documents would you like to analyse and why?

- How could you ensure that your report is not biased?

- What problems do you expect to encounter? And how will you overcome them?

- What are the limitations of your outcomes and findings?

The case study

Yin (2003) says: 'The case study is valuable when a why or how question is being asked about a contemporary set of events over which the investigator has no control.'

The researcher seeks to elucidate the unique features of a case – organization; person; location; event. A case will try to illuminate decisions – why were they taken?

Who took them? When were they taken? How were they implemented? By whom and why them? And with what result? It is very difficult to generalize from a case study but a strong link to theory either supporting or not, as the case may be, is essential. Case studies do not control the variables. They study variables or phenomena in their own settings.

The case study method is often used for studying organizations undergoing change. You can look at change retrospectively as well as in real-time analysis. Looking at the history behind why and who etc, the change that took place or is taking place are very important as part of the story of the case and its current situation. We can see the reasons why certain things happened and who or what caused them to occur and who or what affected them. This is considered to be causal interpretation of processes and situations.

They are also useful where theory or previous research is still at a formative stage.

Stake (2006) talks about three types of case study: the intrinsic case where you are trying to understand a unique issue; the instrumental case where you are looking at a larger issue and looking for insight; and the collective set of cases which are combined into one study – multiple cases to illustrate the issue.

Cases can be exploratory or explanatory. That is, you are either seeking to explain a phenomenon or trying to explore an issue and the type of research questions you ask will guide you on this.

Your cases will focus on being either *exploratory,* where the main questions you ask will start with *What?*, or they could be *explanatory* where the question tends to begin with *How? Why? Who?*

All cases are likely to include some descriptive elements where you will ask *Where? When?*

How many case studies do you undertake?

This is a question that is always asked. How many cases do I need to find? The answer is not easy as it all depends. Sometimes one case is sufficient and sometimes a small number of related cases is required. You need, however, to focus in on a rounded analysis with a good analysis of related factors. Richness of detail is more important than numbers. You are looking for cases that are typical and will provide useful understanding.

Cases may be chosen to compare or contrast – replication is where the same results of your analysis will be expected for all your cases; this could be where you expect the same results as the cases are so similar; or it could be that the results would be similar as there are similarities in the cases.

If you can only find one to use – or you are required to only use one case as that is the organization for which you are undertaking the work, then you will need also to make an argument about why only using one case is enough. You might say: 'Well, this case allows me to test a very significant theory.' Or you might say: 'No one has been able to access this organization before for research purposes.' Or: 'This is a unique or rare case.'

If, however, you are using more than one case, then you must make an argument as to why this is required. You might say: 'I need more than one case as I need to see if I will get exactly the same result when I analyse the material – I will collect the data in exactly the same way' – this is literal replication; or you might say: 'I need more than one where I will collect the data identically as I suspect for these reasons ____ (state them) that I will get similar results;' or 'I will get different results which I can explain due to ____ (this theory).'

Yin (1994) says that the results are 'yet more potent if two or more cases support an equally plausible rival theory' (p 31). The evidence from multiple case studies is often more compelling and thus can be regarded as being more robust.

It is suggested that your case study findings should be generalized to theory, not to other cases – and thus the theory becomes the vehicle for examining these cases. Obviously this will be the theory that you have discussed in your literature review.

Where do your data come from in case studies?

The first place you will need to look for data is within the case organization itself. You need to access as much relevant archival material as you can. This might include annual reports, committee reports, analyses of the topic you are studying in internal reports or memos.

There are a number of potential issues here that you need to be aware of when collecting these data. Can you, for instance, collect all this material? Some material may not be available to you for privacy or security reasons; others may not be made available to you for reasons of internal politics. Some may, of course, be already shredded or archived in such a way that it cannot be accessed. If you cannot access all the material, will you obtain a biased viewpoint of the situation?

The second place for documents will be in grey and publically available literature. So look on the web – many organizations will place reports and annual reports on the web; you can look in newspapers and professional journals; you can look in consultancy reports. But always be aware that anything that is placed on the web may have been heavily edited by the organization before being made accessible; or that reporting by a journalist or consultancy etc may have a bias and thus should not be taken as completely accurate. Be a little bit cynical about all such material!

Other types of physical data you can use are multimedia. Few students take enough advantage of the possibilities that our media-rich age affords them. Why not take photographs of the work situation when looking at how software works, for instance? Why not look at office layout and draw it? Why not use any YouTube videos that the organization has made?

Using deductive theory in case studies

Normally speaking, when researchers – and that includes you, my reader – speak about case studies, there is an inherent assumption that the research design will follow an inductive test of theory.

However, Bitektine (2008) has argued that it can also be used for deductive theory testing. He says that by using what he calls a 'prospective case study design', where the researcher 'formulates a set of theory-based hypotheses in respect to the evolution of an ongoing social process and then tests these hypotheses at a pre-determined follow-up time' (p 161), a deductive case study will follow. The test can be carried out by pattern matching as used by a number of authors (see Campbell, 1966 and Trochim, 1989). The pattern matching is relatively simple – it requires, according to Trochim (p 360), 'a theoretical pattern of expected outcomes, an observed pattern of effects, and an attempt to match the two'. Variables will therefore be explicitly stated with hypothesized values and operationalized in the data collection.

The lessons learnt from the first case will be applied to the second and subsequent cases to match and perhaps adjust where the patterns do not match.

Another deductive method is called the 'alternative theoretical templates strategy'. Here alternative theories are applied to a single case to contrast the assumptions, explanations and thus recommendations. It uses a true/false method of testing theories to see if applying a different theory will give a different explanation (eg in ICT implementation there are different theories to explain why people might refuse to use the new software, ranging from usability to political power plays).

Cross-sectional case study design

This type of design collects the data that occur naturally – usually on several cases at a single point of time (less than a year), to detect patterns of association in variables. It is often called a social survey and may use questionnaires but typically also incorporates semi-structured interviewing and document analysis.

Cross-sectional design is interested in more general findings than a case study. It differs from comparative case study design in that it typically looks at multiple (small) cases whereas comparative will only look at two.

Longitudinal case study design

This is used to map change over a period of time in years. The data will be collected at least twice at different times on the same case organization. It can look, for instance, at household spending habits and compare 1950 with 2000. Usually this type of secondary data will be collected from databases such as in the social housing survey discussed, but it can also interview the same people in an organization before and after a change management programme has been implemented.

Note that it is possible to combine more than one approach as long as you can justify it. If it will achieve your aims and you can make the argument, then you can undertake the research in the way that you choose to.

Denzin's Triangulation says that if you can combine more than one approach to look at and analyse the data then you have triangulated the data. This verifies your results.

Triangulation is particularly useful in case study research as you will likely be evaluating a number of activities within the case; and you may be looking at complex or controversial issues. Triangulation also gives a broader perspective.

So, according to Denzin (see Denzin and Lincoln, 2005), you can look at your case across time – if you should have more than a few months to study an organization – say 9–12 months; or across levels, eg interviewing singly or in groups or at different levels in the organization; additionally you might consider different theories as to what is happening within the case and analyse for these different theories.

An exploratory case example:

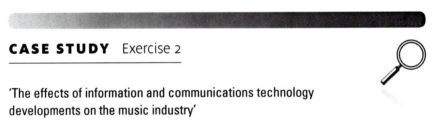

CASE STUDY Exercise 2

'The effects of information and communications technology developments on the music industry'

- How would you develop a good case study project – assuming that this is your title?

- Would you need one or more than one case to undertake this? Why? What would you expect from your study if you looked at one case against more than one?

- What information would you require?

- What sources would you use to acquire data and what might be the issues relating to the collection of these data?

- Would there be any ethical issues in relation to undertaking this project? If so, what? And how would you ensure that all ethical codes are adhered to?

- What type of contribution to knowledge do you think this project might make?

An explanatory case example:

CASE STUDY   Exercise 3

'The emergence of standards in the telecommunications industry'
   The above is the title of your project.
   In order to undertake this project you will require a sponsor organization
and you have acquired a significant sponsor who is heavily involved in regulating
the telecommunications industry.

- How would you now develop a good case study-based project?

- What information would you require?

- What data would you need? And how would you collect these data?

- What issues do you think you might encounter? And do you think you might
  attempt to overcome them?

- Would there be any ethical issues that you would need to consider?

- What type of contribution to knowledge do you think this project might make?

Case study tactics adopted for design quality (an example of justifications from an article)

TABLE 7.1 Enhancing the rigour of qualitative research: application
of a case methodology to build theories of IT implementation

Criterion	Description	Adopted tactics
Construct validity	Establishing correct operational measures for the concepts being studied	Multiple sources of evidence Review of case study report by key informants Mix of qualitative and quantitative methods

Criterion	Description	Adopted tactics
Internal validity	Establishing a causal relationship, whereby certain conditions are shown to other conditions, as distinguished from creating spurious relationships	Explanation-building strategy with logical chain of evidence Review of case study report by key informants Site analysis meeting Sufficient citations in the case report Checklist matrices Tying propositions to existing literature
External validity	Establishing the domain within which a study's findings can be generalized	Analytic generalization Tying propositions to existing literature
Reliability	Demonstrating that the operations of a study can be repeated, with the same results	Validation of coding scheme Case study database Case study protocol

References

Bitektine, A (2008) Prospective case study design, qualitative method for deductive theory testing, *Organisational Research Methods*, 11, 160–80

Campbell, DT (1966) Pattern matching as an essential in distal knowing, in KR Hammond (ed) *The Psychology of Egon Brunswick*, Holt, Rinehart and Winston, New York, 81–106

Denzin, NK and Lincoln, Y (eds) (2005) *The SAGE Handbook of Qualitative Research*, SAGE Publications, London

Stake, R (2006) *Multiple Case Study Analysis*, Guildford Press, Guildford

Trochim, WMK (1989) Outcome pattern matching and program theory, *Evaluation and Program Planning*, 12, 355–66

Yin, RK (1994) *Case Study Research: Design and Methods*, Sage, Thousand Oaks, California

Yin, RK (2003) *Case Study Research: Design and Methods*, Sage, UK

08
Collecting data: less common methods

Multi-methods and multi-sources lend rigour to research.

One thing that is worth noting is that by using a combination of methods and methodologies – both quantitative and qualitative, deductive and interpretivist – and also different methods for collecting specific types of data, you can add a layer of rigour to the analysis of the data.

By combining interviews with surveys or interviews with social network analysis, for instance, you are looking at specific types of data that are more sophisticated and can be considered more reliable.

In this chapter we introduce you to some methods for collecting data and some elements of how to use them for analysis that can add a level of sophistication and reliability.

Specifically, we cover:

- social network analysis;
- action research;
- the Delphi method;
- participant and non-participant observation;
- using crowdsourcing; and
- the repertory grid.

Questions you will be able to answer after completing this chapter:

- Will my research have improved rigour by using a combination of methods?

- Which combination of methods would be most appropriate for my project?

Key points that you should take away from this chapter are:

- There is no one right way to collect data and analyse them, but using multi-methods in a project to collect data can highlight previously unknown or undiscovered relationships that affect how the data are interpreted;

- Using multi-methods provides the triangulation that Denzin says is required in a good project.

Mixed methods research

Properly used mixed methods research is a design methodology, a paradigm, and not just an arbitrary mix of qualitative and quantitative techniques.

Margaret Adolphis

Definitions

Grafton *et al* (2011), in their literature review of mixed methods research in accounting, identify two components as key to mixed methods: integration of methods, and the fact that the research should concern a single study or programme of enquiry (as opposed to parallel studies or programmes).

Johnson and Onwuegbuzie (2004, p 17) offer a similar definition: 'mixed methods research is formally defined here as the class of research where the researcher mixes or combines quantitative and qualitative research techniques, methods, approaches, concepts or language into a single study'.

In his definition, Cresswell (2007, p 5) talks about underlying philosophical assumptions that guide the collection and analysis of data, and the 'collection, analysis and mixing of data'. His central argument is that '...the use of quantitative and qualitative approaches in combination provides a better understanding of research problems than either approach alone'.

Resources include the *Journal of Mixed Methods Research* and in 2005, the *International Journal of Social Research Methodology* ran a special issue (Issue 3) on mixed method research.

Social network analysis

This is both a data collection method and an analysis method rolled into one.

It is a method for studying the social interconnectedness of individuals in any group. It can be performed in an office, for instance, to discover who is the central person with specific knowledge, or to find the unacknowledged leader. It can be used in a social space such as looking at friendship patterns on Facebook. It can show the flow of information around an organization. It can reveal who talks to whom and who doesn't get contacted by anyone.

It therefore has a multitude of possibilities within both qualitative and quantitative research as an additional tool to add layers to the data collected and inform the analysis.

We use social network analysis methods to work out the adjacency matrix – which can be the strength of times a particular person is mentioned perhaps – or who uses a number of terms in common. It uses comprehensiveness, density and centrality measures, eg density being the number of links present/number of potential links.

One example is of an office where there are 100+ employees. A simple e-mail survey was sent to each employee asking who they turned to when they had a technical problem, and in what order they would ask the first three of these employees (see work by Coakes and Smith). The results demonstrate the people most respected by their colleagues as being technical experts. The arrows indicate in which direction the questions were posed. So if you look at person 101, you see two arrows are pointing towards him, indicating that two people would ask him questions, but he has no arrows heading outwards, so he asks no questions of anyone else. This would indicate that he has some limited specialist knowledge that he does not need to ask others about, or that he is very isolated from his colleagues and perhaps does not know what they know. The opposite would be person 06 right in the middle of this diagram, who has many arrows heading in towards him indicating that a lot of people think he has specialist knowledge that they require, and also has a number of arrows heading outwards showing that he does ask questions of others.

If you use variations of this analysis you can discover not only what skills people have but also where friendships lie and many other interesting connections between people.

If you do use social network analysis then you will need to look up the specific methods for analysing and these are given in books such as Knoke and Yang (2008).

Action research

One of the most common research methods used for data collection when undertaking internal change projects is that of action research.

It is very commonly used to change behaviour and to test hypotheses about how the behaviour can be changed. It looks at the varying relationships between different entities. It is an instrumental study in which the researcher seeks 'to consider their original research propositions and hypotheses in the light of experience, modifying, reformulating and rejecting them, adopting new hypotheses' as required (Reason, 1994, p 327). It is frequently used for problem solving.

Although it uses hypotheses for undertaking the change management, it provides textual data that will then need to be analysed with a qualitative method. This can make it difficult to undertake and often people need specific training in this method before undertaking projects using it. It is a method of research for the confident researcher, as although it tests hypotheses, the project is not fully planned in advance but rather evolves as each action is reflected upon.

Questions about action research:

- What are the most common situations in which action research is undertaken?

- What are the main methods that are used by action research and how do I undertake an action research project?

- What are the most common pitfalls that can be encountered by action research?

Key points that you should take away from this section are:

- Action researchers believe that the world is a fishbowl and is undergoing constant change. The researcher and the research are part of and are instrumental in this change. As we research, we change the world around us. We plan, we act, we observe, we reflect.

- In action research we are attempting a conscious change in the world in which we are acting and we do this within a single organization at any one time. It is not possible to conduct action research in several organizations at the same time.

- We must monitor and reflect on the results of our action as it is these reflections that form our next hypothesis and next action within the project.

- It can be considered part of the sociotechnical paradigm, with the participants in the project providing feedback as the project progresses, and their feedback forming part of the data that we reflect upon before the next action is taken. Thus stakeholders help design the project.

- It is essential to fully and completely understand the environment in which the action research is to be undertaken before embarking on such a project.

- It is a type of small-scale intervention in the real world. It examines the result of that intervention, and is concerned with diagnosing problems in a very specific context, and attempting to solve the problems in *that* context. It is thus very situational:

  - First you diagnose the problem.

- Then you undertake the therapeutic element – ie you undertake a direct change experiment.
- Then you observe, reflect and decide next move and the cycle continues until the end of the change experiment.

When to use action research

- As a spur to action – to get things done quickly.
- To address some kind of personal functioning, eg job efficiency, personal motivations, relationships.
- Job analysis to improve functioning.
- Organizational change.
- Planning and policy making.
- Innovation and change within existing and ongoing systems.
- Problem solving.
- Opportunity to develop theoretical knowledge.

How do you start?

- Identification, evaluation and formulation of the problem.
- Preliminary discussions among affected parties.
- Review the literature for a student project.
- Consider the problem statement – does it need modifying?
- Select research procedures – sampling and administration.
- Select evaluation methods.
- Implement.
- Monitor with questionnaires, diaries, interviews etc.
- Interpret results.
- Reflect and start next cycle.

Action research is very flexible, due to the ability to change direction at the end of each cycle as circumstances direct, but it is also very difficult to isolate the influencing factors.

Potential problems with action research

- In an organization, it may be considered as a political ploy.
- It is very context specific and thus cannot generalize.
- It can lack precision and control.
- It can be difficult to duplicate due to individual circumstances and context.
- It can be difficult to write up.

If you do decide to go with action research then it is important to consult specific texts and journals that look at issues and how to undertake this type of work. Some examples are given in the References section on pages 143–145.

Exercise

Looking at the example given below, can you list at least three potential influencing factors that my student had not considered?

An example:

One of my students was teaching at an infants' school in an area of the world where the children in her class had been in refugee camps before they came to her. In these refugee camps they had been deprived of play toys and equipment and had very little opportunity to run around, jump and play physical games.

She noted that their reading and writing and arithmetic scores were far behind those of the average child of their age. She also noted that their coordination skills were rather poor.

Reading the educational literature about how she could improve their skills she found that some theorists likened physical coordination skills to academic skills, such that an improvement in physical coordination could lead to an improvement in academic skills.

Considering this she felt that it would be a worthwhile experiment to see if the improvement of her students' physical coordination would lead to an improvement in their academic skills.

She therefore set up an action research project whereby she would be the researcher and enactor and the children would be the participants.

The children were first tested on both their academic skills and physical coordination skills against some recognized accepted levels for their ages.

She then asked the children how much playing and what type of playing they had undertaken in the camps and recorded their responses in her log.

She then devised some games for them to play – starting with very simple physical skills such as ball games and running and climbing.

At the end of the week she asked the children to record in their diaries what they felt about the games and their ability to concentrate on academic work and also interviewed them again and recorded their responses. She retested them with the same tests and recorded any changes.

Each week she did this, and each week she devised new additional skill challenges for the children to undertake on an individual level, depending on how they had improved their scores. She reflected on each set of results in her log.

At the end of the set period – in this case one term – she completed the experiment with a final set of diaries and tests and interviews.

All the materials she collected during this term, including her reflective diary, formed part of her data to analysis. She then analysed her data in a traditional qualitative text manner and wrote up her report, including comments and statements from the children's diaries demonstrating how they had changed and also included her reflective log as an appendix.

Some answers:

- family background and position in family of child;
- nutritional background;
- emotional issues due to refugee status;
- parents or lack of them;
- any underlying physical impairments due to malnutrition or lack of medical treatment in camp or before;
- cultural background;
- previous home environment and economic status – eg social class and family money.

How to... carry out Action Research: www.emeraldinsight.com/research/guides/methods/action_research.htm?PHPSESSID=pmn9sfc t8ieo1u4u0lga7ff9u5

This article defines and situates it, then looks at how to design a good action research project, how to ensure its validity, and the best vehicles of dissemination. Finally, it looks at some useful sites on action research.

Delphi method

The Delphi method is a group facilitation technique that seeks to obtain consensus on the opinions of 'experts' through a series of questionnaires. It is a useful communication tool to systematically collect and aggregate informed judgements from a group of experts on specific questions or issues (Helmer, 1977; Reid, 1988). Researchers employ this method primarily in cases where judgemental information is indispensable.

The initial questionnaire may also collect qualitative comments, which are fed back to the participants in a quantitative form through a second questionnaire. At the end of round one, the researchers review, judge and capture the information from experts' responses and compile the results into the second iteration. In the second round, each participant is then able to take into account the opinions of the other participants when responding to the second round of questions (Daniel and White, 2005). The process continues until group consensus is achieved or a predetermined point in the process is reached.

Dalkey and Helmer (1963) state that the method obtains the most reliable consensus of a panel of experts by putting them through a series of in-depth questionnaires interspersed with controlled feedback. This technique is different from brainstorming or other group approaches, as its process is non-threatening and anonymous, avoiding (group) interactions of individuals, but helping experts express their opinions freely.

The Delphi method has been used in various areas, but it is a particularly popular method in identifying critical factors requiring expert judgement (eg Holsapple and Joshi, 2000; MacCarthy and Atthirawong, 2003; Xiao et al, 2006).

For example, it was employed in identifying barriers to knowledge transfer in organizations (Sun and Scott, 2005) and factors affecting the location selection decision of an international operation (MacCarthy and Atthirawong, 2003). It has also been used in strategic planning (McKnight 1991); theory and design applications (Corotis and Harris, 1981); the future of inter-organizational system linkages (Daniel and White 2005); rural tourism project evaluation (Briedenhann and Butts, 2006); and the selection of procurement systems for construction (Chan et al, 2001).

Identification of experts

A Delphi study 'doesn't depend on a statistical sample that attempts to be representative of any population' (Okoli and Pawlowski, 2004, p 20). It is a group decision mechanism requiring qualified experts (Okoli and Pawlowski, 2004). Therefore, the key to a successful Delphi study mainly lies in the selection of participants, who are knowledgeable and willing to contribute (Gordon, 1994).

Delphi survey administration

To collect a wide array of views, the first round of the Delphi survey is usually qualitative, using open-ended questions allowing experts to elaborate freely in their responses (Linstone, 1978).

Content analysis is used to analyse the panel's feedback and group the factors according to similar themes.

In the second round of the survey, the number of instances that fell into each category is counted and the frequencies of factors are fed back to panellists in descending order. The experts are also given their previous answers to remind them what they had said in the first round.

Evidence in the literature shows that either two or three rounds of surveys are preferred (Beech, 1997). When considering the level of consensus to be required, it is argued that a universally agreed proportion does not exist for the Delphi method, as the level used depends upon the sample numbers, aim of the research, and resources. Based on Loughlin and Moore's work (1979), McKenna (1994) suggested that consensus should be equated to a 51 per cent agreement among respondents.

Participant and non-participant observation

Participant observation

(Adapted from: Danny L Jorgensen (1989) *Participant Observation: A Methodology for Human Studies*, Sage)

Jorgensen says in this book that participant observation is suitable for research when a number of factors are present. These factors include that the:

- research problem is concerned with meanings and interactions as seen from the insider's viewpoint;
- investigation can be undertaken within normal day-to-day life;
- researcher can gain access to the setting;
- setting is a case – it is limited in size and location;
- research questions are suitable for case study work; and
- qualitative data collection by observation is relevant and will provide insight that cannot be gathered by other means.

Participant observation is especially appropriate for exploratory studies, descriptive studies and studies aimed at generating theoretical interpretations. Though less useful for testing theories, findings of participant observational research certainly are appropriate for critically examining theories and other claims to knowledge.

Jorgensen further says that there are seven requirements that must be met:

1. there must be a special interest in human meaning and interaction as viewed by an insider for a particular setting;

2. there must be a location in the here and now of a particular setting which then provides a foundation for the inquiry and use of this method;

3. that the theory used will concern interpretation and the understanding of human existence;

4. the inquiry must be open-ended, flexible, opportunistic, and will constantly redefine and reflect on the problem being observed;

5. that this will be an in-depth case study using suitable qualitative research methods;

6. that the participant will be able to maintain relationships with the others in the setting; and

7. that direct observation will also occur alongside other methods of data collection. These will include documents of all types; communications including audio, photographic and TV where

appropriate; and also artefacts such as clothing, materials and tools of the trade. Participant observers also gather data through casual conversations as well as interviews and questionnaires.

Additionally, DeWalt and DeWalt (2011) say participant observation usually requires the observer to live in the context for a period of time; to learn and use the local language and dialect including any specific terminology and acronyms etc; to actively participate in the daily routine and all other activities of their community; to use the opportunity of conversation as interviews; to actively observe when relaxing with their community; to record all observations assiduously; and to use both tacit and explicit information when analysing and writing up.

And Cargan (2007) adds that the goal of the participant observer is to be invisible in that role. They should appear to be part of the community and not visible as a researcher: 'Participant observation seeks to uncover, make accessible, and reveal, the meanings and realities that people use to sense make in their daily lives. It does not begin with a theory or hypothesis.'

If you are to be invisible to your community, then perhaps you are to be considered a covert participant observer – if you have not made your intentions plain when you join the group, this can be a stressful role but permits very close engagement with the community; otherwise you are an open participant observer. If you are an open participant observer, then your role as a researcher will be known to all in the community.

There are two other possible researcher roles: they are non-participant but also can be either covert or open.

The covert non-participant is hidden from view – perhaps behind a one-way mirror as in police stations when interviews are being carried out. A concealed camera could also be recording behaviour for later analysis. This is an ethical dilemma for the researcher even though 'true' behaviour is being recorded. Is it right to observe people without their knowledge? And then to use this observation to record and write about them?

The open non-participant is in a different situation. Here you have permission to watch and record, perhaps by videoing in a corner while office work is carried out around you. Perhaps by acting as a shadow as someone carries out their day-to-day tasks. Initially, the person or people being watched will act unnaturally, but as time progresses they will forget you are there and normal behaviour will ensue.

How to use crowdsourcing as a research tool

(Information below adapted from the Emerald website: www.emer-aldinsight.com/research/guides/methods/crowdsourcing.htm?PHPSE SSID=pmn9sfct8ieo1u4u0lga7ff9u5)

What is crowdsourcing, why is it used and how does it work?

Crowdsourcing involves three elements:

1. A problem or task is assigned to a wide, and random, audience (the crowd), rather than a selection of experts.

2. The crowd then generates shared content on a voluntary basis (although there may be some small payment), which may be data to resolve a particular problem (for example, Galaxy Zoo where people are asked questions about images), or a collection of memorabilia associated with a particular community (for example, East London Lives, which documents the effects of the Olympics on the lives of East Londoners).

3. The above activities are facilitated by online technology.

Howe recently wrote a book (2008) which examines online examples of crowdsourcing from the business and scientific worlds and would be a useful resource.

Why use crowdsourcing?

- Why use the crowd rather than experts?
- Why should people volunteer their time to provide content to a website when it is so much easier just to browse what is there?

A cynical response to the former question is that it comes down to funding. Goodchild (2007), in discussing the phenomenon of volunteered geography, claims that citizen input to mapping helps fill a hole created by the decline in government-funded mapping (p 217).

The challenges of funding, as well as the ease with which anyone can upload content to the internet, have, according to the UK's Joint Information Systems Committee (JISC), changed the way in which online collections are created and used (JISC, 2010).

There may, however, be genuine statistical reasons why the crowd, because it is naturally diverse, performs better than experts. Take prediction – when the disparate guesses of a large number of people are averaged out, the results are often better, and more accurate, than that of an individual expert.

It's a phenomenon which has been used by researchers at George Mason University to study ways in which crowdsourcing can help in intelligence gathering.

And, in some cases, the crowd may have better knowledge than the expert. According to Goodchild (2007), locals may be able to provide early warning of natural disasters because they are familiar with the area, while satellites only pass infrequently.

As to why people volunteer their time, one explanation is the desire to contribute to the common good, and to gain recognition from others, as is the case with the academic community (JISC, 2010, p 7).

Upshall (2011) suggests other reasons: interest in the subject, ease of contribution, and some form of reward, which may or may not be financial.

How to use a repertory grid

(adapted from Emerald):

The repertory grid – an overview

The repertory grid is a way of carrying out an interview in a highly structured manner, using the interviewee's own language and setting out their responses in the form of a grid.

ect

and Joshi, KD (2000) An investigation of factors that
management of knowledge in organisations, *The Journal
Information Systems*, 9(2), 235–61
) *Why the Power of the Crowd Is Driving the Future of
rown Business*, New York, NY
and Dick, P (2001) A social constructionist account of police
its influence on the representation and progression of female
repertory grid analysis in a UK police force, published in
n International Journal of Police Strategies & Management,
–99
Joint Information Systems Committee, Capturing the Power of
and the Challenge of Community Collections, available at:
.ac.uk/publications/jiscinform/2010/~/link.aspx?_id=0ED8E52
28B38E24FA31C8E9A4&_z=z, accessed January 24th 2012
and Anthony, J Onwuegbuzie (2004) Mixed methods
a research paradigm whose time has come, *Educational
er*, October 2004, 33(7), 14–26
55) *The Psychology of Personal Constructs: Volumes One and
utledge, London
and Yang, S (2008) *Social Network Analysis*, Second Edition,
ndon
HA (1978) *The Delphi Technique* Westport, Connecticut,
ood
K and Moore L (1979) Using Delphi to achieve congruent
ves and activities in a pediatrics department, *Journal of Medical
tion*, 54, 101–106
hy, BL and Atthirawong, W (2003) Factors affecting location
ons in international operations – a Delphi Study, *International
al of Operations & Production Management*, 23(7), 33–45
a, HP (1994) The Delphi technique: a worthwhile research
ach for nursing, *Journal of Advanced Nursing*, 19(6), 1221–25
ht, J (1991) The Delphi Approach to Strategic Planning, *Nursing
agement*, 22 (4), 55–57
C and Pawlowski, SD (2004) The Delphi method as a research tool:
xample, design consideration and applications, *Information and
agement*, 42(1), 15–29
, PE (1994) *Participation in Human Inquiry*, Sage Publications,
don
N (1988) *The Delphi Technique: Its Contribution to the Evaluation
Professional Practice*, Chapman & Hall, New York
YT and Scott, JT (2005) An investigation of barriers to knowledge
nsfer, *Journal of Knowledge Management*, 9(2), 75–90

A big advantage of the repertory grid technique is that it allows interviewees to articulate their experience in the way they see the world, according to their own personal constructs. It avoids interviewer bias and because it uses differences and similarities with other examples, it can be easier to tease out the interviewee's views.

The repertory grid technique, therefore, can be a rich source of qualitative data and allow people to express things in their own terms or jargon. Because it also uses rating scales, it can also be analysed statistically, hence it combines both qualitative and quantitative methodology.

Kelly developed the repertory grid technique based on his theory to enable structured conversations between researcher and participant and explorations of the individual's world of meaning. Unlike standard approaches to research, such as questionnaires and interviews, the repertory grid can elicit people's constructs without influencing them by the researcher's preconceived questions.

The main components of a repertory grid:

1. The topic – what the interview is about.

2. Elements – these are examples that illustrate the topic. They can be people, objects, experiences, events, according to the topic. The elements can either be chosen by the interviewee, or they can be preselected.

3. Constructs – the most important component of the repertory grid. This is where the elements are compared with one another to produce a series of statements which describe what the interviewee thinks about the topic. These statements will form the eventual unit of analysis. They will be bipolar – in other words, every statement will be presented as opposite ends of a pole.

4. Ratings – once the main constructs and elements are in place, they are entered on a grid with the elements on top and the constructs down the side. The interviewee then rates each element against each construct according to a rating scale, usually of 1–5.

Uses of a repertory grid

Because of its ability to capture good data, the repertory grid is used in a wide range of contexts. For example:

- human resources (eg performance appraisals, job analysis, training needs analysis, staff and organizational development);

- psychology (for example, psychological tests or counselling-type interviews);

- brand analysis and consumer behaviour;

- team development and organizational studies; and

- information retrieval studies and systems analysis.

For example, suppose a student is asked about their experience of lectures. The interviewer might ask, 'What makes a good lecturer?' If the student struggled to respond, the interviewer might give a couple of prompts, perhaps based on his or her conception of what qualities a good lecturer should possess. With the repertory grid technique, the student and the interviewer could agree on a range of particular lecturers and then use a technique of comparison and contrast as a way of getting the student to talk.

It is particularly good in circumstances where it is important to understand how people think, for teasing out knowledge that is implicit rather than explicit, and for establishing mental maps.

Advantages and drawbacks of a repertory grid

- It is time-consuming; each interview will take up to an hour.

- It can appear rather artificial, and senior managers in particular may be sceptical about its value, and hence rather unwilling to give time to it.

- There are many variations of design and it can be difficult to select the right one.

- The analysis process can 'overwhelm with numbers' and one can become fascinated by the process of computer analysis and what it can 'discover' – at the expense of the 'bigger picture'.

 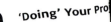

References

Adolphis, M, How to... use mixed
emeraldinsight.com/research/gui
SESSID=pmn9sfct8ieo1u4u0lga7

Beech, BF (1997) Studying the futur
disciplinary clinical staff view the
mental health centres over the cou
Advanced Nursing, 25, 331–38

Briedenhann, J and Butts, S (2006) A|
to Rural Tourism Project Evaluatio
171–90

Cargan, L (2007) *Doing Social Resear*
Maryland, US

Chan, APC, Yung, EHK, Lam, PTI, Tam
Application of Delphi Method in sele
construction projects, *Construction M*
699–718

Coakes E, and Smith PA, (2007) Commu
Supporting Innovation, *Journal of Kno*
The Knowledge Garden, Vol 8, Special
com/jkmpv8si107.htm

Corotis, RFR and Harris, J (1981) Delphi M
applications, *Journal of the Structural Diu*

Creswell, JW and Clark, VLP (2007) *Design*
Methods Research, Sage, Thousand Oaks,

Dalkey, N and O Helmer, O (1963) An Experi
Delphi Method to a Group of Experts, *Man*

Daniel, EM and White, A (2005) The Future (
System Linkages: Findings of an Internation
Journal of Information Systems, 14, 188–20

DeWalt, KM, DeWalt, BR (2011) *Participant C*
Fieldworkers, 2nd edition, Altimira Press, Ply

Goodchild, MF (2007) Citizens as sensors: the v
geography, *GeoJournal* , 69, 211–21

Gordon, TJ (1994) The Delphi method, *Futures*
1–33

Grafton, J, Lillis, AM, Mahama, H (2011) Mixed
accounting, *Qualitative Research in Accountin*
5–21

Helmer, O (1977) Problems in futures research: de
impact analysis, *Futures*, February, 17–31

Holsapple, CV
influence tl
of Strategic
Howe, J (200
Business, (
Jankowicz, D
culture an
officers: A
Policing,
24(2), 18
JISC (2010)
the Crow
www.jisc
9910541
Johnson, R
research
Research
Kelly, G (1
Two, R
Knoke, D
Sage, L
Linstone,
Green
Loughlin
objecti
Educa
MacCart
decisic
Journ
McKenn
appro
McKnig
Man
Okoli,
an e
Ma
Reasor
Lor
Reid,
of
Sun, I
tra

Upshall, M (2011) 'Crowdsourcing for education', paper presented to Online Information 2011, 29 November–1 December, Olympia National Hall and Conference Centre, London, available at www. online-information.co.uk, accessed 23 January 2012

Xiao, J, Douglas, D, Lee, AH and Vemuri, SR (2006) A Delphi Evaluation of the Factors Influencing Length of Stay in Australian Hospitals, *The International Journal of Health Planning and Management*, 12(3), 207–18

09
Ensuring data saturation

The question students always want answered is: 'When will I know that I have enough data?'

Initially, of course, it will be answered by your research design and the sampling regime that this has set up. (Setting up a research design framework, see page 26 onwards.)

With quantitative data it is quite easy to decide as:

1. there are some definitive studies which indicate how many responses will indicate a valid statistical inference;

2. statistical techniques indicate this through – for instance – (as mentioned by Malhotra and Dash, 2010) the use of the standard deviation;

3. there is a minimum sample size for co-relational research for a one-tailed hypothesis is regarded as being 64, and 82 for two-tailed (Onwuegbuzie, and Collins, 2007);

4. for causal-comparative research, a minimum of 51 participants per group for one-tailed, and 64 for two-tailed, analysis.

5. it is noted that precision in these statistics increases steadily as sample sizes increase up to sample sizes of 150–200 (Fowler, 2009).

Validity of quantitative data

This can be both internal and external and is difficult to generalize across time.

Internal validity is normally tested through:

- content – the extent to which the data provides adequate coverage of the investigative questions that guided the study;

- criterion-related validity – which considers the success of measures used for prediction or estimation; or

- construct validity – which attempts to infer abstract characteristics for which empirical validation seems unlikely.

Reliability of quantitative data

It is also necessary to consider the reliability of the data – which supports the validity of the outcomes.

In order to test data reliability there are a number of standard tests that can be used – the 'gold standard' being Cronbach's Alpha. (If you are not sure what this test is, then check it out in your statistical textbook, or the YouTube (how2stats, 2013) references given – but to note that it is the corrected item–total correlations and the inter-item correlation matrix.)

Significance of quantitative data

Having assured ourselves that the data are both reliable and valid, it is then necessary to consider significance.

Significance is tested through either parametric (or conventional), or non-parametric means.

- Do the data supply consistent results?
- Were the data free from random or unstable error?

Nominal and ordinal data are tested through non-parametric means. To ensure correctness in assumptions, it is very easy to test for the use or not of parametric tests through looking at a distribution plot of the data. If they fall into a normal distribution – say a bell curve or along a straight line – then a parametric test is required; if it isn't a normal distribution, then tests such as the Chi-Square – which can be used for most non-parametric situations (Blumberg *et al*, 2008) – should be used. (Again if this test is unfamiliar to you, you need to look at your statistics textbook or the following videos – Eisenberg, 2010; EducatorVids, 2011).

With qualitative data it is not so clear.

It will depend on how the research design says that the data will be collected.

As the most common route for qualitative data collection is through interviews, we will consider those first.

In setting up the research design a sampling frame will have been decided upon and for interviews this can be done in a number of ways.

The most common is often what we call snowball sampling – whereby you interview all the people concerned with a particular project or activity, asking each for other people to interview. When only the same names are repeated and you have interviewed them all, then clearly data saturation has been achieved.

An alternative route to snowball interviewing that is very common is to choose one person to represent each type of stakeholder in the project or activity. In which case, if you have chosen and interviewed a representative sample, again saturation will be achieved.

What becomes more difficult is when there is not such a nice easy framework to work with.

Suppose you want to interview female managers about their experiences of the 'glass ceiling' effects. How will you know when you have enough?

Here we can turn to some studies that have been undertaken and quote a recognized expert – for instance:

- Bertaux (1981) says that the smallest acceptable sample size in qualitative research is 15.

- Guest *et al* (2006: 78), in examining a sample, found that 'data saturation had for the most part occurred by the time we had analysed 12 interviews' and for most research enterprises, in which the aim is to understand common perceptions and experiences among a group of relatively homogeneous individuals, 12 interviews should suffice.

- Romney *et al* (1986: 326) say that in situations of well-informed individuals that are in a homogeneous culture, as few as four respondents can produce a high level of accuracy and well below 30 is a reliable sample.

- Kuzel (1992: 41) says six to eight interviews for a homogeneous sample and 12–20 data sources 'when looking for disconfirming evidence or trying to achieve maximum variation'.

- Marshall (1996: 524) says that in a purposive sample of physicians, thematic saturation was evident after about 15 interviews and theoretical saturation occurred after 24 interviews.

So we can see that while there is no absolute clarity as to the number necessary, it can be argued that somewhere between five or six and 15 interviews would be suitable for most postgraduate work, although clearly one would expect more if a) the interviews were short; and b) the study was part of a PhD programme (see Mason, 2010) .

It is for you, the student, to justify your sample through theoretical means, thematic saturation (see analysis of qualitative data section), or through using quotes such as those above from reliable authors who discuss these data saturation matters. See the list of references below for some indication of where you should be looking for these.

References

Bertaux, D (1981) From the life-history approach to the transformation of sociological practice. In Bertaux, D (ed) *Biography and society: The life history approach in the social sciences*, Sage, London

Coyne, IT (1997) Sampling in qualitative research. Purposeful and theoretical sampling; merging or clear boundaries? *Journal of Advanced Nursing*, 26

EducatorVids2 (2011), Statistics: Chi Square Goodness of Fit Test: www.youtube.com/user/EducatorVids2?v=PnU1nNLRt4k&feature=pyv, accessed March 2013

Eisenberg JD (2010) Simple Explanation of Chi-Squared: www.youtube.com/watch?v=VskmMgXmkMQ, accessed March 2013

Fowler, F (2009) *Survey Research Methods*, Sage Publications, London

Guest, G, Bunce, A and Johnson, L (2006) How many interviews are enough? an experiment with data saturation and variability, *Field Methods*, 18, 59

How2stats Chronbach's Alpha Part 1 (spss): www.youtube.com/watch?v=2gHvHm2SE5s (accessed March 2013)

How2stats Chronbach's Alpha Part 2 (spsss): www.youtube.com/watch?v=9rS49o1rdnk (accessed March 2013)

Kuzel, A (1992) Sampling in Qualitative Inquiry, in Crabtree, B and Miller, W (eds) *Doing Qualitative Research*, Newbury Park, CA, Sage

Malhotra, NK and Dash, S (2010) *Marketing Research: An Applied Approach*, Dorling Kindersely, Pearson Education South Asia

Marshall, MN (1996) Sampling for Qualitative Research, *Family Practice*, 13

Mason, M (2010) Sample Size and Saturation in PhD Studies Using Qualitative Interviews. Forum Qualitative Sozialforschung / Forum: Qualitative Social Research, 11

Onwuegbuzie, AJ and Collins, KMT (2007) A typology of mixed methods sampling designs in social science research, *The Qualitative Report*, 12(2), 281–316

Romney, AK, Batchelder, SC and Weller, WH (1986) Culture as consensus: A theory of culture and informant accuracy, *American Anthropologist*, 88, 313–38

Sandelowski, M (1995) Sample Size in Qualitative Research, *Research in Nursing & Health*, 18

PART THREE
Reporting your findings

10
Analysing quantitative data

This chapter is designed to introduce you to the potential quantitative methods for data analysis and the tools that can help with this analysis.

The most common introductory tool that can be used for quantitative data analysis is Excel; more complex data analysis can be undertaken with the SPSS software program and this software is available to use within most universities should you wish to take advantage of it.

This chapter will remind you of some of the simple statistical techniques that are most commonly used and their purposes.

If you intend to use statistical analysis then you are most likely to be working in a positive paradigm and to be using hypotheses that your data will test. A positive paradigm implies that you will express a relationship between variables; state these in an unambiguous form; and imply the possibility of empirical testing. There will be independent and dependent variables.

Your choice of which statistical technique or procedure to use will depend very much on how you intend to utilize these data – is this the prime source of data? In which case it is likely that you will need more in-depth analysis – and you will then need to consider whether or not your data are parametric. If your analysis is confirmatory, then you will be looking to draw conclusions from a sample to a population and again more powerful tests will be required. While charts are of interest to the reader they are not considered to be prime tests of quantitative data and analysis of this type of data needs to go beyond simple averages or percentages.

Questions you will be able to answer after completing this chapter:

- How do I select the most appropriate method for analysing my quantitative data?
- Do I understand the most common methods of quantitative analysis?
- Can I interpret the results of simple quantitative analyses?

Key points that you should take away from this chapter are:

- Quantitative data are very useful to confirm theory testing when a suitable size of sample can be provided.
- Primary quantitative data are usually collected through a survey but unless surveys are collected internally in an organization they can be tricky to populate, that is to obtain sufficient participants to make statistical analysis valid.
- It is possible to analyse secondary data, such as large existing datasets, with quantitative methods.
- It is possible to combine qualitative methods with quantitative and this is most suitable when the sample population from which the data can be gathered is too small for significance testing, eg combine interviews with an internal organizational survey.

Why should you undertake statistical analysis of data?

- to judge the quality of the work presented to you;
- to assess the content to develop further hypotheses
- to be able to pass critical judgement – have the statistical methods been correctly used?
- to ensure supporting arguments for the research are based on valid work;
- to verify the internal reliability of the samples used and presented;
- to support the method used as being appropriate to the data collected and the hypotheses used;
- to ensure that the samples were representative;

- to distinguish between statistical significance and relevance – to ensure that the result is not significant but meaningless!

When looking at data that have been collected for statistical analysis, the first and most obvious method of analysis is by using Excel to provide simple graphs and percentages, means, averages etc. Word can also be used to illustrate these data in tables.

Data can be categorical, ie they describe a category such as gender, colour, favourite food and so on; or quantifiable such as height, age, portions of fruit per day.

Data can also be classed as: nominal; ordinal; interval; and ratio. See Table 10.1, which describes these data.

We can also illustrate these data in tables which give the categorical type and a simple frequency. See Table 10.2 below. Table 10.3 gives an illustration of a two-way frequency table and Table 10.4 demonstrates a grouped frequency table.

You can also use standard charts for describing your data such as bar charts; pie charts; histograms; and scatter plots.

TABLE 10.1 Data description

Types	Description
Nominal	No scale or order, eg location, gender
Ordinal	Ordering but no scale, eg sun cream use
Interval	Order and scale but no sensible zero, eg temperature
Ratio	Ordering scale and sensible zero, eg age, height

TABLE 10.2 Categorical type and simple frequency

Favourite food type	Frequency N	Percentage %
Carbohydrate	272	40
Protein	15	23

(Continued)

TABLE 10.2 *(Continued)*

Favourite food type	Frequency N	Percentage %
Dairy	151	22
Fruit and vegetables	97	14
Total	673	100

TABLE 10.3 Two-way frequency

Favourite food type	Male %	Female %	Total %
Carbohydrate	121	253	374
Protein	25	28	53
Dairy	68	97	165
Fruit and vegetables	44	59	103
Total	100	100	100

TABLE 10.4 Quantifiable – grouped frequency

Height (Metres)	Frequency (N)	Percentage (%)
120–129.9	9	1
130–139.9	13	2
140–149.9	62	9
150–159.9	222	33
160–169.9	233	35
170–179.9	102	15
180–189.9	32	5
Total	673	100

FIGURE 10.1 Column chart example

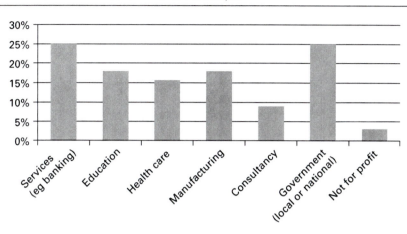

FIGURE 10.2 Horizontal bar chart

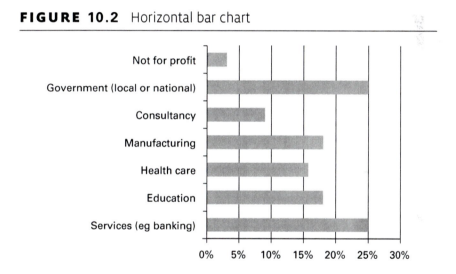

FIGURE 10.3 Pie chart

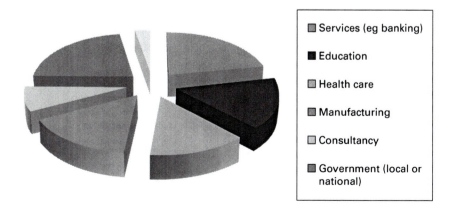

FIGURE 10.4 Scatter chart along an axis 1

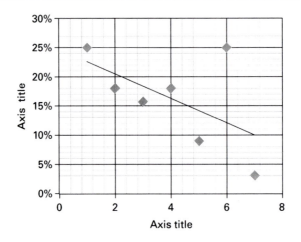

FIGURE 10.5 Scatter chart along an axis 2

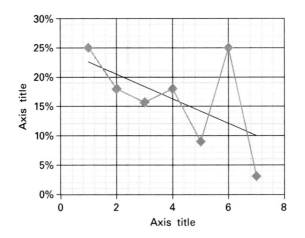

FIGURE 10.6 Pie of pie chart

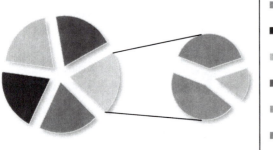

FIGURE 10.7   Radar chart

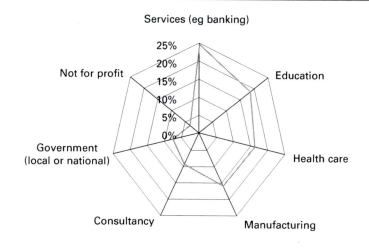

Measures of central tendency

These are simple measures that indicate how homogeneous the range is. A bell curve indicates that the data are homogeneous and fall exactly either side of the mid point.

It is important to choose the most relevant according to data type, eg mean for height, and also according to the shape of the frequency distribution.

Exercise data:

Services (eg banking)	25%
Education	18%
Health care	16%

TABLE 10.5   Simple measures of central tendency

Measure	What it stands for
Mean	Sum of all numbers and divide by n (the total of numbers in the range)
Median	Middle value (numbers)
Mode	Most common (number)

FIGURE 10.8 Example chart

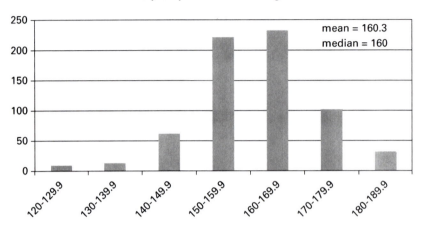

Frequency distribution of height

mean = 160.3
median = 160

Manufacturing	15%
Consultancy	9%
Government (local or national)	8%
Not for profit	3%

For the exercise above, work out what is the:
Mean = ? ; Median = ? ; Mode = ?

Measures of spread

The main measure is that of a range from maximum to minimum; standard deviation; quartiles; and the inter-quartile range.

A standard deviation converts the variation into a number, and the greater the number the greater the spread between top and low numbers. Here in Table 10.6 we can see that one student got 0 and one student got 76. The standard deviation is thus very large and possibly unrealistic. For more realistic statistics we would take out the 0 as this is likely to be a student who did not attend. Any student that did attend but did not complete any work at all could

TABLE 10.6 Example: marks for a student exam

	36
	0
	20
	52
	68
	48
	20
	80
	56
	24
	72
	72
	76
Average =	49
Stdev =	25.42
Median =	54
Mode =	68

be given 1 to indicate that they got no marks for any work but did attend.

Quartiles are the three values in a dataset that 'divide' the data into four 'equal' parts. The difference is the inter-quartile range.

FIGURE 10.9 Quartile values

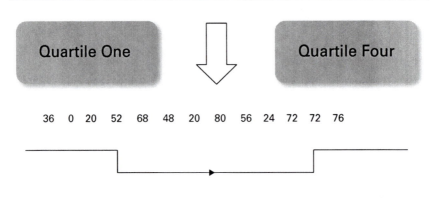

Quartile One ⬇ Quartile Four

36 0 20 52 68 48 20 80 56 24 72 72 76

Some notes on statistical testing

When considering the data collected you also need to think about how you intend to analyse the results. Having chosen to consider quantitative data you now need to consider how to test the data for reliability and validity as well as to discover whether or not they support your hypotheses.

Nominal data such as gender, and ratio data such as age in years, are reliable in and of themselves, so you need to consider ordinal and interval data to determine greater or lesser value, or the equality of intervals or differences.

Validity of data can be both internal and external and as your data may be difficult to generalize across times etc you may be concerned with internal data validity. Internal validity is normally tested through content – the extent to which the data provide adequate coverage of the investigative questions that guide the study (Blumberg, Cooper and Schindler, 2005); criterion-related validity, which considers the success of measures used for prediction or estimation; or construct validity, which attempts to infer abstract characteristics for which empirical validation seems unlikely.

You then also need to consider the reliability of your data – which supports the validity of your outcomes. Do the data supply consistent results? Are the data free from random or unstable error? In order to test your data reliability there are a number of standard tests that can be used. The most common chosen to use are: Cronbach's

Alpha; Spearman–Brown Prophecy formula with the Split–half Correlation; and the Kuder–Richardson Formulas 21 and 20 to overcome the known deficiencies in the Spearman–Brown test.

Having assured yourself that your data are both reliable and valid you need then to consider – are they significant? (As a reminder, as we have discussed this before.) Significance is tested through either parametric or non-parametric means. Nominal and ordinal data are tested through non-parametric means, which indicates that so should our data as we are largely considering ordinal data. However, to ensure that you are correct in your assumptions it is very easy to test for whether or not you should use parametric tests through looking at a distribution plot of your data. If they fall into a normal distribution – say a bell curve or along a straight line – then you must use a parametric test, if it isn't a normal distribution, then you should use instead tests such as the Chi-Square, which can be used for most non-parametric situations.

Cronbach's Alpha

When the items on an instrument are not scored right versus wrong, Cronbach's Alpha is often used to measure the internal consistency. This is often the case with attitude instruments that use the Likert scale. A computer program such as SPSS is often used to calculate Cronbach's Alpha.

Split–half

A total score for the odd-number questions is correlated with a total score for the even-number questions (although it might be the first half with the second half). This is often used with variables that are scored 0 for incorrect and 1 for correct. The Spearman–Brown prophecy formula is applied to the correlation to determine the reliability.

FIGURE 10.10   Split–half reliability testing

$$\text{Reliability of scores on total test} = \frac{2 \times \text{reliability for ½ test}}{1 + \text{reliability for ½ test}}$$

Kuder–Richardson Formula 20 (K-R 20) and Kuder–Richardson Formula 21 (K-R 21)

These are alternative formulas for calculating how consistent subject responses are among the questions on an instrument. Items on the instrument must be scored 0 for incorrect and 1 for correct. All items are compared with each other, rather than half of the items with the other half of the items.

Figure 10.11 indicates the tests available for reliability.

FIGURE 10.11   Reliability testing

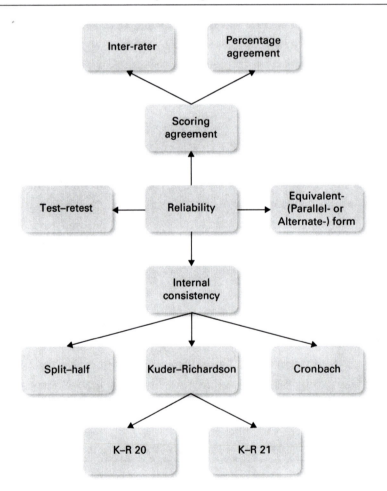

Reproduced with permission from Del Siegle

Siegle, 2009

If the results excluding non-responses can be treated as a binomial distribution (the binomial distribution is often used to model the number of successes in a sample of size n drawn with replacement from a population of size N. Note that sampling schemes may be without replacement – where no element can be selected more than once in the same sample; or with replacement where an element may appear multiple times in the one sample. For example, if we catch fish, measure them and immediately return them to the water before continuing with the sample, this is with a replacement design, because we might end up catching and measuring the same fish more than once), then we calculate statistical confidence levels with a degree of validity.

A confidence interval is a type of interval estimate: the use of sample data to calculate an interval of possible (or probable) values of an unknown population parameter. A population parameter is one that indexes a family of probability distributions where you assign a probability to each of the possible outcomes of a random experiment. It can be regarded as a numerical characteristic of a population or a model, in contrast to point estimation, which is a single number of a population parameter and is used to indicate the reliability of an estimate.

Cross-tabulation is a statistical process that summarizes categorical data to create a contingency table. It is heavily used in survey research, business intelligence, engineering and scientific research. It provides a basic picture of the interrelation between two variables and can help find interactions between them. This is important when considering hypotheses and variables and deciding whether such variables are dependent or independent.

Cross-tabulation leads to the following contingency table:

TABLE 10.7 Contingency table from cross-tabs

Participant	Age	What KM training have you undertaken?
1	20–30	On the job
2	20–30	In-house courses

(Continued)

TABLE 10.7 (*Continued*)

Participant	Age	What KM training have you undertaken?
3	20–30	On the job
4	20–30	On the job
5	30–40	University degree in KM
6	30–40	On the job
7	30–40	External courses run by training companies
8	30–40	None
9	40–50	None
10	40–50	On the job

TABLE 10.8 Totals from cross-tabs

Row labels	20–30	30–40	40–50	Grand total
External courses run by training companies		1		1
In-house courses	1			1
None			1	1
None		1		1
On the job	3	1	1	5
University degree in KM		1		1
Grand total	4	4	2	10

Variables: dependent and independent

Dependent variables are normally expressed as y; independent are expressed as x.

Thus we can obtain an expression of y = f(x).

How does y change when we vary x? – where y is the variable we are interested in.

Deconstruction exercise: to form hypotheses

Statement: In the UK, tall people have a better chance of gaining high rank.

TABLE 10.9 Stage 1 of deconstruction

Tall people	Have
Male/female	Over what time?
Age(s)	Historical change?
Birthplace	(Had?)
Socioeconomic status	
Height	

Gaining	A better chance
Duration of career	Statistical confidence
Length of service	Comparison with whom
Positions held	Appropriate statistics (rationale)
Progress	
Training?	

In the UK	High rank
In other countries	Measured by?
Is company based in UK?	£/perks/number of subordinates/
Is company international?	company size/company turnover/
	organizational chart
	Industry
	Commerce
	Service

FIGURE 10.12 Stage 2 – Making the links

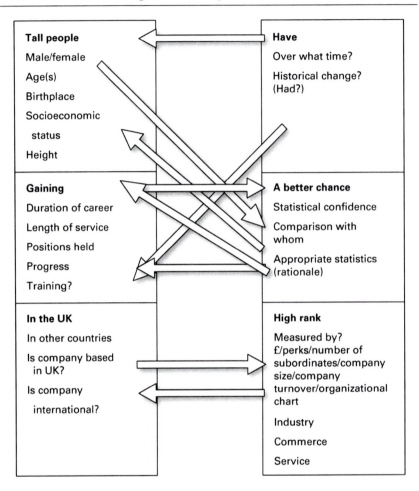

You can of course, add more and more links to each part, of each part, of the statements as you investigate further.

The statement is deconstructed. This means that the various elements in it are specified and selected to form the hypotheses. The arrows show the links that can also be made for further hypotheses. Remember that these hypotheses are then used to collect data and each will link to a question or questions in your survey.

So Stage 1 hypotheses are:

- A tall male is more likely to gain high rank in the UK.
- A tall female is more likely to gain high rank in the UK.
- An older person is more likely to gain high rank in the UK.

And so on...

- A person may gain higher rank in the UK if they have been in their job for a longer time.

- A person who has had a longer career is more likely to gain high rank in the UK.

Stage 2 hypotheses will therefore become:

- Tall people in the UK with a long career are more likely to have more subordinates, which indicates that they have a higher rank.

Where you make the links between the two sides of the deconstruction table.

References

Blumberg, B, Cooper, DR and Schindler, PS (2005) *Business Research Methods*, McGraw Hill, Maidenhead

Cooper DR and Schindler PS (2006) *Business Research Methods*, McGraw Hill International, New York

For more information on all the above statistical methods of analysing your data you need to look at a statistical handbook such as *Statistics for Surveys* and also consider the following websites for explanations:

Exam Solutions have a full series called Making Maths Easy: www.youtube.com/watch?v=wNamjO-JzUg considers the Median and the Quartiles

Siegle D (2009) looks at reliability and validity: www.gifted.uconn.edu/Siegle/research/Instrument%20Reliability%20and%20Validity/Reliability.htm

Statistics For Surveys: www.youtube.com/watch?v=YHXadaW_lso&feature=related

Introducing statistics from book chapter 1 [perdisco.com/perdiscotv]; chapter 2 = presenting; and 3 = measuring; 4 = probability; 5 = more probability distributions; 6 = sampling; 7 = estimation; 8= hypothesis; 9 = comparison; 10 = regression

Using SPSS for more advanced work: try the how2stats videos: www.youtube.com/watch?v=Wlk2QPIa2f8&feature=relmfu

Additional videos are available for other SPSS work from same organization

11
Analysing qualitative data

The purpose of this chapter is to look at the issues of text, and related data collected by qualitative means as research data, and how we codify this text and data so that we discover (hidden) meanings or are able to compare like data with like data. In short, we need to be able to analyse textual as well as numeric data to make sense of them.

We need to make sense of textual data, sift them, organize them, catalogue them and select the themes that emerge for discussion in our analysis and our findings from our research. These textual data are not just the data we collect from our subjects that we may interview but are also the textual data that we collect along the way including the literature we read – articles and books – and other secondary data such as reports and memos from our case organizations etc. All textual data can be analysed to provide us with themes and meanings for discussion. In this we include any 'text' that is collected from artefacts including video and photographs as their contents can be considered text for this purpose.

There are a number of challenges to analysing qualitative data, including:

- reducing the total amount – which could consist of hundreds of pages of interview textual output;
- structuring the data other than in a chronological manner so that sense can be derived; and

- providing the data in a form that can be easily understood – including diagrams or models where appropriate.

We will demonstrate in this chapter some of the most commonly used formal methods of textual analysis that will assist in surmounting some of the challenges identified above – so that our final report for our project is fully justified when the textual data are included.

Questions you will be able to answer after completing this chapter:

- How can I demonstrate an understanding of different methods of analysing qualitative data?

- How can I demonstrate a capability to analyse qualitative data?

Key points that you should take away from this chapter are:

- Reading textual data is an active activity – we read to comprehend and facilitate analysis.

- Data are encountered as a messy corpus that we organize into themes and these themes are later incorporated into our discussions to provide the basis for our arguments.

- Data and their social reality are two different entities and must be considered as such and distinguished as such in our arguments.

- Textual data meanings and sense making are largely emergent and are not usually easily distinguished on the first pass through the data but will require multiple passes of sense making in order to discover the 'truth' of the data.

- Textual data enrich numerical data and encourage a deeper understanding of social realities.

We need to consider briefly the study of what signs mean. What are their social connotations? Why is some language particular to one social group? And why do people use different language when talking to different people?

Using the holiday analogy, we often see that different cultures use different gestures from our own. For example, do you shake your head up and down or from side to side to indicate 'Yes'? Is it polite to belch at a meal? Do you clear your plate to indicate you are happy with the meal and are finished? Or do you clear your plate to indicate you want more?

If you are talking to a child, do you use different language from when you are talking to an adult? And have you noticed how many people talk really slowly and loudly in their own language (often the English, truth be told) to try and get non-native speakers to understand a request?

When we write up this study and analysis we frequently use a thematic description of the study, as the textual data are organized into themes – or categories – and build an understanding of the data that may lead to either confirmation of the initial proposition or development of new or alternative theoretical explanations for the situation under examination and the behaviour within it.

Coding text

We will demonstrate in this section one of the most commonly used formal methods of textual analysis that will help surmount some of the challenges identified above – so that our final report for our project is fully justified when the textual data are included. This is sometimes also called content analysis.

How do you start?

You start by reading, reading again, and then reading again.

The first time, you read thoroughly and try to make sense of the text (this also applies to any audio or visual 'text'). The second time, you look at the text and start to highlight what seem to be important items. Annotate alongside to indicate why you think they are important. The third time, you read through and check your annotations and highlights. Have you missed any? Do your justifications make sense? What linkages do you begin to see?

At this stage you can take the text and assign each file/document a name and number; each page a number; each paragraph on each page a number; and each line a number within that paragraph.

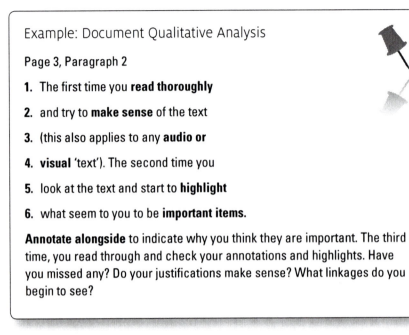

Example: Document Qualitative Analysis

Page 3, Paragraph 2

1. The first time you **read thoroughly**

2. and try to **make sense** of the text

3. (this also applies to any **audio or**

4. **visual** 'text'). The second time you

5. look at the text and start to **highlight**

6. what seem to you to be **important items.**

Annotate alongside to indicate why you think they are important. The third time, you read through and check your annotations and highlights. Have you missed any? Do your justifications make sense? What linkages do you begin to see?

The act of numbering begins to break the text up into chunks. The highlighted words and phrases are your first attempt at coding the document. Remember:

- each code needs to be identified by its location within a document;

- each code will be considered as to whether it links to other codes; and

- each code will also be compared to other documents and texts you are looking at to ensure that each time you see the same words or phrases they are all assigned the same code.

So, looking at the text in the example above, we have highlighted the following words and phrases: 'Read thoroughly'; 'make sense'; 'audio'; 'visual'; 'highlight'; 'important items'; 'annotate alongside'.

We have two major codes here: 1) instructions; and 2) type of text.

Instructions include: 'Read thoroughly'; 'make sense'; 'highlight'; 'annotate alongside'.

And type of text is 'audio' and 'visual'.

'Important items' is a reminder to you!

We could link the phrases within the codes to indicate some causality – ie if you read thoroughly, highlight and annotate alongside, it is likely that you can make sense of the data.

So, in the document qualitative analysis, on Page 3, in Paragraph 2 we have two codes identified: type of text is in lines 3 and 4; and instructions are in lines 1, 2, 5, 6, and 7. We note these codes down in a separate document with all the necessary details as we have done above.

This stage is also called open coding. This allows us to look back at these codes and where we defined them for future texts and permits us to compare and contrast the definitions.

Once we have completed analysing all the documents/texts we can look at all the codes we have identified. This stage is called axial coding. In this stage we consider whether we can put the codes together differently and what the links between the codes are – again we might consider causality here as being a link. We look for themes and patterns and consider whether our definitions are correct or need adjustment. What are the relationships between codes? Can we now see codes in the documents that we had missed but need to fill in? Codes are usually classified as:

- descriptive codes = manifest codes;
- analytical codes = latent codes = themes, topics, concepts; and
- axial codes = relationship codes.

We can display some of these themes as diagrams or models. Below we show different ways of displaying these linkages.

What you will be aiming to do is to demonstrate the importance of your findings (to the organization being studied, to research, to the people under observation etc) in a format that can be easily understood, which is where these types of models or diagrams are useful.

Whether or not you code by hand or through a computer-based tool (see below where we discuss some of these), once you start coding, your data become fragmented and thus can be difficult to trace back to their origins when you need to reference them (the document number, page, paragraph and line numbers may be needed for direct quotations). Thus we strongly recommend that you keep records of

FIGURE 11.1 A mind-map diagram which demonstrates the links to organizational cultures and human/barriers within an organization to the sharing of knowledge.

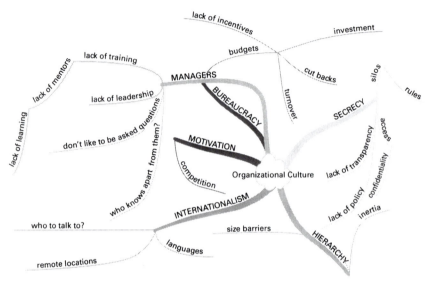

(Taken from: Coakes, Amar and Granados, 2013)

your documents on perhaps a spreadsheet listing the document numbers, names, dates of acquisition, origin etc. We then recommend that you make more than one copy of the documents so that they can be sorted in different manners. For instance, you may want to look at all reference documents from your organizational archive by year, origin, department, content and so on so that you can track things through by different dimensions and causalities. This may be separate computer files or physical files – this is your choice as to which way you work best. Ensure that all transcripts of interviews have a locked read-only copy as well as copies where you code the data. That way when you want to include quotes from your interviewees, you can always go back to their exact words. Always keep an audit trail of what you have coded and why to check on and to produce for your appendices.

Checking

One thing we strongly recommend is that you check a sample of your analysis with a friend. Give them one page of one of your transcripts that has some significance to you, and ask them to code it for you – open coding – and perhaps look for causality. You will need to choose someone ideally from your course or who has the same degree background as you. Then check what they code against yours. You are looking for around 75–80 per cent consistency in coding. This is known as inter-rating and should be written up in your research methodology and data analysis sections as it is important to note that they have coded the same as or similarly to you. This adds to your verification of your analysis. Even if you are a subjective analyser – which all qualitative people are – you will need to attempt to justify your results and inter-rating is one verification method. The other verification that you will demonstrate is during your write-up of this section, where you will ensure that you lay out each stage that you went through with examples demonstrating it very clearly. You should ensure that your appendices include an example of a coded transcript/document and the full tables of codes and causality links.

The example below shows how codes could be demonstrated when undertaking observation as a research method:

TABLE 11.1 Codes from observation

Field Notes	Codes	Themes
I entered the Tube station and passed through the barrier gates. I then looked for how I could access the platform. I found that there was a directional arrow to the nearest lift. However, it then failed to tell me that this lift was 100 yards away when the nearest staircase was five yards and was only five steps deep.	Access Directions Failure (to consider possibilities/ alternatives)	Accessibility Diversity of disabilities

Issues with coding

There are a number of issues with coding that might raise their head and that inter-rating might make apparent.

These include the fact that no two researchers will ever code exactly the same. This is because coding is largely subjective and based on an individual world view. Just as no one's knowledge will be exactly the same as anyone else's, their understanding of that knowledge will also differ.

There is also the issue of time. It takes time to complete a research project and over time the researcher's understanding of knowledge and thus of their data may change. Thus the coding may also change. This is why the reasons for each code being given at the time of coding must be kept up to date, so that they can be checked against the new codes.

This leads us to the point that when these new codes do appear and then it seems that some data were coded incorrectly, or at least not with the same codes for the same reasons, and this will upset a theory that was being developed or a concept or causal mapping, then there is a potential for a researcher to try and 'force' data into codes that are not correct by the new understanding. This must, of course, be avoided and is one reason for making sure that you have sufficient coding time available after data collection. While data collection may have issues, then coding also may have issues that relate to time.

Causal mapping

Causal mapping can be performed on text of any sort. It can be quantitative or qualitative but is more often the latter – see above discussions on causality when looking for connections between codes.

There is a point of redundancy when you no longer get any new concepts from the data – if you still get new concepts then you need to go back and collect more data.

Causal statements imply cause and effect. Look for these words and phrases in the text:

Explicit key words – 'if–then'; 'because'; 'so'.

Implicit key words – 'think'; 'know'; 'believe'.

Separate your statements and concepts into cause and effect.

A raw causal map will give:

| Causal statement | | link | | Effect statement |

'so'

Individual causal maps can be aggregated:

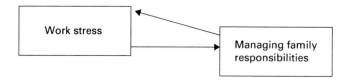

Which is the effect and which is the cause?

While you are analysing the textual outcomes of interviews or additional related documents, as part of your causality analysis, you can count the times certain words or phrases occur in the documents and speeches.

This counting will help identify the words or phrases that reoccur and thus have most emphasis put upon them in the minds of those using them.

For instance, if during your count of 152 documents with 1,135 statements or words that seem to you to be significant, you find that financial decision making and its related terminology are mentioned less than 50 per cent of the time in relation to strategy say, then you can identify how important the concept of financial decision making is, and what causality it may have in relation to strategy. You could develop a tree or model of the most important statements/concepts/phrases according to the percentage of times used to illustrate this.

Software for coding

You can be helped by using software if you prefer rather than coding by hand. The most well-known software for coding is NVivo, now version 10. It is software that supports mixed methods as well as qualitative research. You can use it to analyse interviews and focus groups; audio and some survey work as well as social media and videos such as YouTube (www.qsrinternational.com/products_nvivo.aspx).

NVivo handles many types of data, including Word, pdfs, pictures, database tables, spreadsheets, audio files, videos including YouTube, social media data and web pages. It can interchange data with other applications such as Word, Excel, SPSS, Survey Monkey, EndNote and Evernote. And it handles several languages as well as English – French, German, Spanish, Portuguese, Simplified Chinese and has a separate Japanese interface. Your conclusions, query results, models and charts can all be exported or simply copied and pasted into reports and presentations.

See also:

1. HyperRESEARCH™, which enables you to code and retrieve, build theories and conduct analyses of your data. With multimedia capabilities, allowing you to work with text, graphics, audio and video sources. Also HyperTRANSCRIBe for the transcription elements of your work: www.researchware.com/products.html.

2. The Ethnograph 6.0: www.qualisresearch.com/features.htm.

3. Atlas.ti, also multimedia and version 7 now out: www.atlasti.com/.

4. See also the following free/open source software:

   - Aquad;
   - Coding Analysis Toolkit;
   - Compendium;
   - QDA Miner Lite;
   - RQDA;
   - Transana;
   - Proprietary software;
   - MAXQDA;
   - QDA Miner;

- Qiqqa;
- XSight;
- Dedoose.

Dedoose and QDAMiner can also be used for mixed method research analysis.

Again, do look on YouTube where you can find a number of training videos for these software programs free of charge.

Causal mapping

There is software that can help with this and concept mapping: www. audiencedialogue.net/soft-visu.html

Plus:

- writedesignonline.com distinguishes five main types of organizers: star/web, chart/matrix, tree/amp, chain, and sketch;
- www.graphic.org has four types: webbing, concept mapping, matrix, and flow chart. They have a table showing how each type can be used for various purposes.

Additionally:

Inspiration is like an outlining program that does diagrams.

Start with a main idea, topic, or issue to focus on. A helpful way to determine the context of your concept map is to choose a focus question – something that needs to be solved or a conclusion that needs to be reached. Once a topic or question is decided on, that will help with the hierarchical structure of the concept map.

Then determine the key concepts. Find the key concepts that connect and relate to your main idea and rank them; most general, inclusive concepts come first, then link to smaller, more specific concepts.

Finish by connecting concepts – creating linking phrases and words. Once the basic links between the concepts are created, add cross-links, which connect concepts in different areas of the map, to further illustrate the relationships and strengthen student's understanding and knowledge on the topic.

- Decision Explorer is another program that expresses concepts in diagram form – designed for working through decisions and their ramifications. Very powerful, but not suited to large chunks of verbatim text. One disadvantage of Decision Explorer is its very high cost, but a free demo version can be downloaded from the Banxia website. It's limited to 60 nodes, which is enough for many small projects.

- Another software package for concept mapping is CMap http:// cmap.ihmc.us/conceptmap.html, as is Compendium, which also has mindmapping and other freeware tools available.

- In addition, there is the FreePlane software: http://sourceforge. net/projects/freeplane/

Other software programs are:

- Omnigraffle, which runs only on Apple Mac.

- Freemind is open-source software for mindmapping, available for Windows, OS X, and Linux.

- Scholonto and Claimaker can be found at kmi.open.ac.uk/ projects/scholonto

- http://sourceforge.net/projects/splmm/ SciPlore MindMapping is based on FreeMind but extended with features.

- www.docear.org/ Docear ('dog-ear') is an academic literature suite. It integrates everything you need to search, organize and create academic literature into a single application: digital library with support for pdf documents, reference manager, note taking and with mind maps taking a central role. It also works seamlessly with many existing tools like Mendeley, Microsoft Word, and Foxit Reader. Docear is free and open source, based on Freeplane, funded by the German Federal Ministry of Technology – highly recommended by a PhD student who tried it for us.

- Freebrain: www.thebrain.com/products/thebrain/

Some interesting articles to read:

Hsiu-Fang Hsieh, Kaohsiung Hsien, Sarah E Shannon (2005)
Three approaches to qualitative content analysis, *Qualitative Health Research*, Vol 15(9), 1277–88.

Content analysis is a widely used qualitative research technique. Rather than being a single method, current applications of content analysis show three distinct approaches: conventional, directed or summative. All three approaches are used to interpret meaning from the content of text data and, hence, adhere to the naturalistic paradigm. The major differences among the approaches are coding schemes, origins of codes, and threats to trustworthiness. In conventional content analysis, coding categories are derived directly from the text data. With a directed approach, analysis starts with a theory or relevant research findings as guidance for initial codes. A summative content analysis involves counting and comparisons, usually of keywords or content, followed by the interpretation of the underlying context. The authors delineate analytic procedures specific to each approach and techniques addressing trustworthiness with hypothetical examples drawn from the area of end-of-life care.

Vincent J Duriau, Rhonda K Reger, Michael D Pfarrer (2007)
A content analysis of the content analysis literature in organisation studies: research themes, data sources, and methodological refinements, *Organisational Research Methods*, 10(1), 5–34.

We use content analysis to examine the content analysis literature in organization studies. Given the benefits of content analysis, it is no surprise that its use in organization studies has been growing in the course of the past 25 years (Erdener and Dunn, 1990; Jauch, Osborn and Martin 1980). First, we review the principles and the advantages associated with the method. Then, we assess how the methodology has been applied in the literature in terms of research themes, data sources, and methodological refinements. Although content analysis has been applied to research topics across the sub-domains of management research, research in strategy and managerial cognition have yielded particularly interesting results. We conclude with suggestions for enhancing the utility of content analytic methods in organization studies.

References

Bauer MW and Gaskell, G (2000) *Qualitative Researching with Text, Image and Sound*, Sage, London

Bazeley, P (2013) *Qualitative Data Analysis: Practical Strategies*, Sage, London

Braun V and Clarke, V (2013) *Successful Qualitative Research: a practical guide for beginners*, Sage, London

Coakes A, Amar, A, Granados, M (2013) Success and Failure in Knowledge Management Systems: A Universal Issue In Series: IFIP Advances in Information and Communication Technology: Grand Successes and Failures in IT: Private and Public Sectors, Editors: Y., Dwivedi, HZ, Henriksen, D, Wastell, and R, De)

Knigge, L and Cope, M (2006) Grounded visualization: integrating the analysis of qualitative and quantitative data through grounded theory and visualization, *Environment and Planning*, 38(11), 2021–37

Ten Have, P (1999) *Doing Conversational Analysis*, Sage, London

Wooffitt, R (2005) *Conversation Analysis and Discourse Analysis*, Sage, London

PART FOUR
Writing your report

12
Discussing project findings

How may students use their findings to address their research question?

Here, the nature and role of a Discussion or Rationale section are presented and how this section may be developed either by extrapolating or interpreting (but not both) students' project findings. A Discussion section is typically presented separately and after a Results section where the data acquired are listed and analysed in the most suitable method according to their type.

Questions you will be able to answer after completing this section:

- How can I extrapolate in a quantitative project?
- How do I interpret the data? What are the methods available to do this?
- What are the pitfalls and disadvantages of each method?
- And what is the rationale for my decision?

Sekaran (1992) says that research is a systematic and organized effort to investigate a specific problem that needs a solution.

Your research has two purposes: 1) to solve a current, existing problem; and 2) to add/contribute to the general body of knowledge in an area of particular interest.

In your discussion you use critical and analytical writing, linking back to theory and to your objectives, to consider what the analyses of your data have shown and what the interesting findings are that contribute to our new understanding and knowledge.

Consider the following:

1. You will need to discuss the significance of your results and whether or not the theory that you have looked at in your literature review confirms the same findings or not. If your findings are different, you will need to consider why they are different.

2. You will indicate what your conclusions are and what evidence you have to derive these conclusions from. These are not the same as the Conclusion section, which is written after this section. Remember you need to draw these findings to a conclusion, which is then repeated in the actual Conclusion section (which includes nothing new). These conclusions that you derive from your results will also be linked to your objectives and your project aim.

3. Was the aim of your project achieved? And did the methods that you used provide this? If you used hypotheses, were they confirmed? If you used qualitative methods of enquiry and propositions, were these propositions useful and correct for your data? Did you develop new theory from your analyses?

4. Was the research design useful and adequate? Would the sample have been improved if you changed or added to it? And how might this affect your results? Might the research have been undertaken by another method? If so, which and why?

5. How might your results be applied to other research or to practice?

6. What questions are there still to answer? So have you solved your problem and have you contributed to knowledge?

If we think about the process of extrapolation as against interpretation, we can see how the two major research designs can differ when we discuss the Results section here.

Ensure that you do not come to what might be termed false conclusions.

This is an oldie but a goodie:

> A boy is in an accident.
> He is taken to hospital.
> He needs an operation.
> The surgeon says 'I cannot operate on him. He is my son.'

What conclusions do you draw? (You should not necessarily conclude that the surgeon is his father, of course, as the surgeon could be his mother.)

Take the next set of propositions:

> **1.** The karate champion is a woman.
>
> **2.** My mother is a woman.
>
> **3.** Conclusion: my mother is a karate champion.

Does 3 necessarily follow from 1 and 2? If not, why not?

> There has been a rise in injuries at work in the sewing factory that was investigated by this research. During the time period investigated, injuries from people pricking their fingers with needles has increased tenfold on the previous two years. Two years before there was only one incident of someone pricking their finger with a needle. It is therefore clear that the rise in injuries is a result of lax behaviour and a lack of care by the staff using the sewing machines. They need to be disciplined every time they prick their fingers and have their pay docked by the cost of the fabric that is ruined due to blood. They would soon learn not to spill blood on the fabric.

Is the conclusion here false or true? Would it work in a factory? And if not, why not? What other alternative conclusions and rationale for the accidents could you supply?

Here is an extract from an interview with one of the workers from this factory:

> When I began at the factory two years ago there were only three people working here and we were all experienced with machine sewing. I had been making dresses for over 10 years with the machine that we then used. However, two years ago, the new owners expanded the factory and brought in 25 new machines and 50 new workers who work part-time only. None of us were trained in how to use these new machines and they are missing a guard by the needle which our old machines had.

What conclusion could now be drawn and what could you infer from what this worker is saying? Can you apply this generalization to other factories? And if not, why not?

Alternatively, here is the report from a survey that was undertaken in the garment sewing district of a large town:

> In our survey of 100 firms in the garment sewing district of X town, we found to a high degree of significance that new machines were regularly bought for these factories. In fact, 75% of these factories bought new machines every five years on average. Of those that replaced their machines sooner than five years, 15% replaced them every two years. In these factories, the incidence of injuries per annum by sewing needles was higher (by 4%) than the incidence in those factories that only bought machines every five years. Our survey participants reported that if they bought machines every five years, operators were able to take longer (by three months on average) to learn to use the machines before becoming fully proficient, and that the owners were able to supply them with longer training courses. They also reported (99%) that only positive rewards (such as bonuses when training was completed on time and to a required standard) affected the injury rate from needles.

Would you be prepared to generalize from this report and findings? Could you extrapolate? (See also the Analysis section for where you would put figures reflecting reliability, validity etc on these percentages.)

Flawed reasoning

Try to avoid the following flawed reasoning mistakes:

1. *Assuming a causal connection.* If two things occur at the same time are they connected? If two things happen in the same place did one cause the other?

For instance, think about yourself and your practice at exam time. Consider the following statement from a typical student: 'I revised very hard for that exam but failed. Next time I will not revise and therefore I must pass.' How true do you think this is likely to be? What reasons for failure from your own experience might there be? And did they really revise as hard as they think they did? What does hard mean in this context? Does it mean more than for other exams? Does it mean more than other students?

2. *Drawing a general conclusion based on one or a few examples.* This is an extremely important point. It is the issue of generalization that has been mentioned before.

You have one case that you have examined. In that case the human resources department decided that by giving everyone a bike they could encourage people to use green transport to come to work. Only 3 per cent of their people used these bikes. The other staff continued to travel to work by their original means of transport. Your conclusion – that bike travel is not a suitable incentive to encourage people to use green transport.

However, you failed to take into account that: 75 per cent of the staff travelled into work by train or Tube as the workplace was situated in central London and most staff lived outside a reasonable cycling distance; and that the remainder of the 22 per cent used buses and pedestrian means of travel. One also used a ferry across the River Thames as he lived on a houseboat.

Beware of extrapolating from too little evidence.

3. *Drawing inappropriate comparisons.* Can you compare the two or more instances adequately? Do they have enough points in common?

Take here an example from my own PhD study.

I had two case study organizations who had agreed to take part in the study. Both organizations were approximately the same size in terms of staffing and turnover. They were both situated in the south-east of England and had been operating for approximately the same number of years. They worked in the same sector and had similar hierarchical structures. Therefore when I began my study I was fairly sure I could compare these two organizations.

However, over time it became clear that although in theory the same organizational structure was in place, in reality in one organization the CEO 'ruled' by charismatic means rather than by position and authority and his process of promotion was by cronyism. Thus the normal rules of hierarchical organizations and how to promote and progress were being broken.

This affected the way staff thought and acted and the two organizations diverged in how they made decisions. One made them strategically through committees and by planning and the other made them almost on whim but certainly according to the desire of the CEO. This thus affected their outcomes. Therefore although I started being able to compare, over time I was no longer able to do so. So the initial points in common remained but the actions differed. What I was able to compare and draw conclusions from was affected.

So in your findings and discussion there are a number of questions that you must answer as you consider the evidence and what conclusions you can draw.

Critical thinking questions:

- Is the evidence that you are looking at actually what it seems to be?

- Could there be other explanations for these outcomes and the analysis drawn from your data, apart from the most obvious?

- Have you got all the necessary data to draw conclusions from? Remember here the limitations on your project and consider how these limitations could affect any outcomes that you see and thus conclusions you might draw.

- Who are your recommendations being made for? If you made recommendations for other parties, would this affect how you looked at the data?

- Can you be certain that there were no hidden agendas or bias in the data you collected – whether from your own assumptions or from your study participants? Remember the potential for suspicion of agendas that they might think you have can affect how people answer questions.

- How reliable are all your data? Be sure that if your data are quantitative that you have fulfilled all the necessary statistical tests for reliability etc. If your data are from interviews, how representative was your sample? And what potential for bias is there as a result?

- If you are using any external data and statistics, have you verified them? Checked their accuracy? Checked any potential for bias in sampling etc? Remember, all your potential failings in data collection may also apply to them.

- Will you consider all the information you have collected? What is relevant to your research question/s and objectives? Do your data analysis and discussion drawing conclusions now permit you to achieve your objectives?

- Does the evidence you have supplied permit you to make suitable recommendations to organizations or practitioners and possibly also academics about the topic area you investigated? Is the line of reasoning from the aim and objectives, to the research design, to the data collection, to the analysis and then the discussion and thus the recommendations from the conclusion, clear and evident to the reader?

Reference

Sekaran, U (1992) *Research Methods for Business: A skill building approach*, Wiley, London

13
Conclusion to your report

What is a conclusion, what is the point of a conclusion, and how does a conclusion differ from a summary?

This final chapter presents the concluding section of a project as the focal point for students to articulate their excitement about their research.

Questions you will be able to answer after completing this chapter:

- How far have my findings matched my original excitement when researching this/these organization/s?

- What are the elements of a strong conclusion? What should be included a) in qualitative projects and b) in quantitative projects, and what should not be included, and why?

- How can I address the typical 'So what?' reaction to student research? Specifically, why would anyone be interested in reading my report?

Here, a number of ways are presented:

In qualitative projects: To convey the student's excitement when researching her organization(s) to other organizations in and beyond her field of interest.

In quantitative projects: To specify what it is that the student has found from her research that constitutes knowledge about the phenomena that the student was originally motivated to research.

How to begin your conclusion

Here are some examples from articles and student work. See if you can spot the difference:

1. Our research question was 'Are HE institutions harvesting knowledge?' The results of our survey showed this was very patchy and indeed hadn't really been considered by some organizations. In addition, their concept of knowledge capture and collection did not necessarily include process sticky knowledge, which is our prime concern here.

2. In our study we noted that KM was embedded in our private sector cases and in some instances had become woven into the fabric of business processes. Where our private sector organizations were more homogeneous with respect to KM our public and voluntary sector cases displayed more heterogeneity in respect of KM. Content analysis of the semi-structured interviews conducted with our respondents leads us to conclude that a trust infrastructure had not been developed in the public and voluntary sector organizations and that as a consequence communities of practice had not germinated and ultimately KM was failing to flourish.

3. We have drawn on the data collected from our two respondents in the charity concerned in order to discuss the extent to which the organization's intranet and its access to the internet provide electronic networks that enable knowledge flows. We have reported the use of such networks to link different sets of stakeholders.

4. The advantages and disadvantages of each distribution channel have been outlined above. The results suggest that, for C***, tied agents will continue to be the dominant sales force. Bancassurance, though without a coordinated strategy at the present, is believed to have the capacity to deliver high growth after the insurer and the bank have achieved synergy. The direct marketing distribution channel in its current condition is unlikely to provide positive profitability for C***. However, the technology involved in this channel may provide a source

of cost saving and efficiency enhancement for the life insurance industry as a whole.

If you answered that 1 and 2 were from articles and 3 and 4 were from students then you would have spotted the difference correctly.

Lessons to be learnt

Lesson 1: There needs to be a sentence which reminds the reader what the study/project was about, eg 'Our research question was...'

Or: 'The/This study set out to...'

You need to link the research question to the findings and the discussion so that you can accurately sum it up and conclude the report.

Lesson 2: This is a summary of your report or study and thus nothing must be included that was not originally set out in your report. Too often we find that new information or literature is introduced into a conclusion to justify a statement. This is wrong and must not happen.

Lesson 3: The conclusion is where you emphasize the contribution to knowledge that your study has produced. Thus you might say that your findings are not consistent with other studies and thus you have contributed new evidence; and then why your study is not consistent – perhaps due to different economic settings of your case study or an age difference in your participants – all of which has already been discussed in your discussion section.

Lesson 4: You need to make a short statement as to what the limitations of your research were and thus what further research is suggested to continue your work. This may be a statement about the lack of time the organization was able to be studied and thus a longitudinal triangulation was not feasible; or that your survey was limited in numbers, eg only 60 participants from one economic sector and thus this may have biased the results and analyses.

Recommendations

The conclusion finishes with a set of recommendations.

Recommendations are what the reader will take forward to their workplace. This may indeed be the organization where you actually work and thus your recommendations will be implemented by management; or it may be other academics who might study this topic or practitioners in your topic area.

So, here is an example of a recommendation. Do you think it is good? If so, will you be avoiding pink food? Or do you prefer another colour? Or, could you write the recommendation better?

> The research suggests that people prefer savoury food to be blue in colour rather than pink. However, as the sample was restricted to people over the age of 60, it is recommended that further research be undertaken with a different demographic group. However, until such research is undertaken, manufacturers of savoury snacks such as those tested in this research should avoid the colour pink when dyeing their food.

14
Reference lists

Projects are required to submit a list of all the references (books, journals, web pages, newspapers, internal reports and so on) they have used to research their study. They are *not* required to submit a list of anything they have read but have not referred to in their text. The first is called a reference list, the second is called a bibliography. Most universities use the Harvard referencing system as this book has also.

The reason supervisors and project examiners require a reference is twofold:

1. They are checking for plagiarism.

2. They are looking for interesting material that you have found, and that they can follow up.

Academics are busy people and do not have the luxury of spending a lot of time reading as widely as they would like. It is very likely that you will be able to find material that they have not yet read and that they would like to read – new views on topics, or new models – and they require the full details so that they can reach this material without a great deal of further searching. Think of your readers and be polite to them by giving them the opportunity to easily read the material you also found interesting.

Remember that most books take some years to make it onto the shelves of libraries or even to be published. Most books also are not leading edge in the topics they are covering but are rather intended for a classroom or background reading.

Nearly all universities will have access to most electronic journal databases in some form or another and it is within these databases that you will find the contemporary debates. Use them carefully and judiciously, and learn to search in multiple ways and through multiple means.

Concentrate your reading on journal articles.

Further specialist reading and resources

Neville, C (2010) *The Complete Guide to Referencing and Avoiding Plagiarism*, Open University Press, UK

Pears, R and Shields, G (2008) *Cite Them Right: The essential referencing guide*, Palgrave Macmillan, Basingstoke

Rules, G (2010) *Harvard Referencing*. Accessed from ukscience. org, Manchester Metropolitan University, Faculty of Science and Engineering, by Rayner, E. and Jones, L, accessed 24 March 2013

15
Writing your abstract

This penultimate chapter ends by discussing an area of a research report that is often poorly thought through by students. Questions you will be able to answer after completing this chapter:

- What is an abstract?
- How can I write (and why should I learn to write) a succinct and eye-catching abstract in a few minutes?

Here are some examples from journal articles and student papers. See if you can tell the difference:

1. This project aims to present some key linkages between intangible assets and social, intellectual and cultural capital drawn from both empirical and theoretical sources. Our empirical study of large UK service organizations was conducted in 2002. We report our findings from 14 case studies where the concepts of intellectual, social and cultural capital have been utilized as analytical tools with which to interpret the data concerned with intangibles.

2. This project defines knowledge and differentiates two specific forms – termed fluid and sticky knowledge. The project shows how knowledge can function as evidence for organizational decision-making. This evidence is comprised of fluid and sticky knowledge, which are used in the cases discussed to underpin

healthcare decisions. Empirical research is used to demonstrate how information and communication technologies (ICTs) are used by one particular UK charity organization in a specific healthcare context. In this organization the ICTs help develop best practice, support virtual communities of practice and assist the lobbying of governments and global organizations.

3. The internet has become an integral and pervasive part of our day-to-day lives. The large corporations are not the only ones using the power of the world wide web to reach out and market their products and services. It is common for smaller organizations, even individuals, to harness the immense possibilities provided by the cyber space.

4. Nearly every big magazine published has an online presence through their exclusive website. It is imperative that all forms of publications learn and follow suit, but with customization based on its target audience.

5. This topic is of keen interest to me as it dwells around my field of expertise – the online space and communities that are involved. ITIL (IT Infrastructure Library) provides a framework of Best Practice guidance for IT Service Management (ITSM). The project focuses on and critically analyses proposals for key improvements in Customer Service and for the Service Desk functions at M***Ltd using ITIL and ITSM frameworks within the constraints of the research. A fundamental question is: how does improving the service desk processes impact on bottom line benefits for the organization? One of the justifications for this project is the increasing competition in the mobile gaming industry.

If you answered that 1 and 2 were journal papers and 3 and 4 were student papers then you were correct. If not, then look again at the writing style and the introductory sentence. (Yes, we cheated by substituting the word 'paper' for 'project'...!)

Lesson 1: Does the first sentence say what the project is about?

It is important to ensure that the person reading the abstract understands immediately what the project is doing, eg 'This project analyses...'

Lesson 2: Do we learn in the next sentence or the following one what research was undertaken? And how? 'By analysing 24 interviews of chief executives of oil companies drilling in the North Sea'; or: 'Empirical research was undertaken with a local health authority and their assistant health workers for the elderly...'

Lesson 3: We need to follow the statement of what research was done, and how and with whom, with a short statement of the research methodology if not already covered, eg case study research, interviews.

We then need to know how many of each type of research, eg one case study, 12 interviews.

Finally, in relation to the research design we need to know whether qualitative or quantitative research was undertaken and what the methods of analysis were, eg statistical analysis using Excel or SPSS was undertaken on the 104 participants of our survey.

Lesson 4: Having introduced what the project was about – what our research question was and how we attempted to answer it – we must now say what we found out. We do not need to include all the results, just the one or two major and important results that have led to new knowledge being created, eg: 'In this organization the ICTs help develop best practice, support virtual communities of practice and assist the lobbying of governments and global organizations.'

Or: 'Our results showed that users were not satisfied with the information and knowledge systems that they were being offered. In addition to multiple technology and usability issues, there were additionally human and organizational barriers that prevented the systems from being used to their full potential.'

Lesson 5: Finally we must state what, as a result of this new knowledge we have discovered, our recommendations must be to organizations, governments or whoever our target audience is.

'Testing the knowledge archetype model, it was found that there were no moderating factors, indicating that a common to all knowledge archetype can be developed for most organizations and thus we recommend that each organization use this archetype to develop such a model.'

Note that there is an alternative version of an abstract that some universities will use. In this version the important items that the students must cover are as follows:

Purpose – Design/methodology/approach – Findings – Research limitations/implications – Originality/value.

You should check with your supervisor and your module handbook exactly what is required in *your* abstract but all the above points will still hold true.

An abstract is placed before a contents list in a bound copy of your project but you should write this last as until the entire project is completed you cannot complete some sections.

You may have a word limit set by your university authorities as to the length of this abstract – you must abide by this limit strictly as too many words will be penalized. It is an exercise in writing concisely.

16
Conclusion

Questions you will be able to answer after completing this section:

- What, in summary, are the main elements of a research project?
- What is the impact of a business research project on the researcher, and how may researchers continue to *enjoy* their business research long after they have finished writing it up?

Key points that you should take away from this chapter are:

- an understanding of two key elements in business research projects that may help to create long-term impact for the researcher in an academic or professional career; and
- a detailed understanding of the main parts in the structure of business projects, and how each part may relate to the researcher's future research and knowledge in, and beyond, academic studies.

The aim of this final chapter is to draw together the main elements of your guide in successfully creating, developing and writing your business project; and to suggest how you may use your experience of completing one of your most challenging assignments in your studies to advance your career, whether this career is in business and management, or in further studies, including a doctorate.

Our rationale for using your research in this way in relating your research to your career, is that in making this connection you will be able to continue *enjoying* your business research long after you have finished writing it up. Successfully using your research to advance your career is the main theme of this concluding chapter, and is what can constitute an important outcome, or *impact*, of your research. (Of course, research impact has a much broader meaning beyond its impact on the careers of individual researchers; but the scope of this book is limited to our consideration of developing good research for your personal enjoyment in and beyond your current business project.) Specifically, we will suggest a number of key elements of your research that you may retain; and how your knowledge of completing your business project will help to distinguish you as a highly employable person, and enhance any future research projects that you may be asked to undertake in your professional work.

Let us first explore what we mean by impact, and then suggest how you may achieve an impact (initially) on your own career from your business research project. Now, assuming that you are reading this chapter after you have at least started to write up your research – can you reflect and recall some of the elements of your project that have helped you to enjoy the research?

Recall that your principal interest in doing your project was to have an opportunity to explore one or more aspects of your favourite business organization(s) or topic. We presented your subsequent process of research as a personal journey in which you were motivated to make meticulous preparations for a trip you were looking forward to making; and we then guided you in following through each stage of your plans in a focused and practical way. As an important motivation for your project was to enjoy your process of research, we suggested how you could learn and apply specific research methods – your working tools – to achieve this objective. Choosing suitable methods and learning how each chosen method may be applied to advance your research were therefore your first requirements before embarking on your business project.

In making your choice of your working tools for research there were two overarching elements that you were advised to learn about and make decisions on, and here we sought to present each of these elements as clearly as possible by relating them to the respective decisions you were required to make.

Principally, we suggested the importance of embedding your work in cutting-edge literature on the topic of your studies so that you may contribute to knowledge of your chosen topic. Now, recall that your topic should concern a field of business studies such as marketing, strategy, HRM, etc and not your research context or the subject of your studies, namely your case firm, where it would be normal to find little information given an abundance of contexts and subjects for researchers to study. The way we have suggested you should draw on literature is by studying the theoretical perspectives that authors use to explain phenomena under study in each piece of literature. Your task would then be to build on existing theory from your chosen literature to address your research question(s), or to draw on a theoretical perspective from another body of literature, as a lens for you to be able to craft a novel and interesting story about your topic.

How may you build, or build on, theory? Let us suggest that the way that you can do so is the way in which you can also contribute to published literature on your topic. This constitutes one of two key elements in producing an impact – your impact from your research – beyond gaining a top mark in your business project. Of course, gaining a top mark is what you want; but you also know that if you have paid for a dream holiday you will not be satisfied if you merely get what you paid for. In your dream holiday you want an experience that you will not forget, an experience that is considerably more than what is described on the label. This lasting memory of your research beyond the mark awarded for your report is what research impact should mean for you in the context of your career – just as your lasting experience of a memorable holiday impacts on your perspective of an enjoyable holiday in any future holidays you may take.

We suggested in Chapter 1 how theory may usefully be viewed as a useful and accurate weather forecast, and as a practical tool to explain a phenomenon and predict its future under a range of possible scenarios (see page 19 onwards). But theory is also different from a weather forecast in that you, the researcher, can alter a forecast from the picture that is portrayed in the literature on your topic if you have data that suggest a significantly different picture from what has been portrayed; *and* if you are able to use your chosen methods of data collection and analysis in weaving a convincing interpretation of your findings. We have already suggested that your ability to meet both these criteria is firstly dependent on the extent to which you are knowledgeable about your chosen literature (Chapter 1). We now want to add to this advice by suggesting that beyond your project, the way that you may use the experience of your research is dependent on your ability to retain your knowledge of the research process.

Specifically, you should clearly record the key steps you took in structuring and developing a high-quality research project without assuming that your experience of this project is an 'academic' exercise that will be forgotten once you leave your business school. Instead of this limited view of 'academic' projects we suggest that you should use the structure of this book as your framework for *all* future research projects, whatever the topic and purpose of this research. Research is research and in respect of the research process there is no fundamental difference in the nature of academic and non-academic (or 'market') research! Let us recall and synthesize the main elements in structuring a research project:

1. A principal RQ (one good RQ should be able to drive a great research project, and sometimes will also drive an entire career's worth of research!).

2. Knowledge of cutting-edge research of your topic – the state of the field – based on academic and market research.

3. Your choice of one or more theories – your weather forecast – for interpreting knowledge of your topic and which you will draw on in addressing your RQ and building new knowledge.

4. Research tools for collecting and analysing data, where the way in which you use off-the-shelf tools is predicated on your choice of methodology.

In this conclusion we want to continue focusing on theory – and your role as a researcher in building theory, given our suggestion that this is one of the two most important learning outcomes of your research project. We have suggested that there exist two different types of theory, and your choice of both types is personal to you. First, theory that you may use to interpret existing knowledge of your topic and address your RQ involves one or more theoretical perspectives developed by business scholars, and we have suggested how you should use theory that you are familiar with. For example, there is nothing 'wrong' with using Porter's Five Forces theory to explain a phenomenon of your research despite the age or popular use of the theory, as the key criterion in using scholarly theory is that you have close knowledge of, and are able to imaginatively apply your chosen theory to explain the phenomenon of interest contained in your RQ, and to predict its possible development pathway(s). (NB: we have set out a number of examples of 'good' RQs in Chapter 1.)

The second type of theory that we also suggest as an important learning outcome for your personal impact is methodology. Here in designing your research we have suggested that you reflect on your personal ontology (your beliefs about what constitutes 'facts' in the world), and epistemology (how and what you choose to define as 'facts'), and make discrete choices between different ontologies and epistemologies.

Assuming that you have made these choices and have conducted your research based on your choices, when you come to write up your research your chosen methodology will then frame the approach you take as well as the language you use in *deducing* specific outcomes of your research. Typically this will be in producing results from testing your hypotheses – or in developing interpretive comments from your *inductive* research that generalize beyond your small sample. The process in which you have drawn, used and developed scholarly theory to address your RQ, and the process in which you have chosen and used your methodology to design your project and conduct your research constitute the two key takeaways from your research project that can have a lasting impact on your career.

In the remainder of this chapter we will examine the possible impact of each part of your project structure on your academic or your professional work. Remember that while each part of your structure is distinct, they should be integrated parts of a single, integrated thought process. Just as in your dream holiday, however many things you want to do and see on your holiday should make little difference to your budget, destination, duration, and other structural aspects of your holiday. In the same way, decisions on individual parts of your project structure – for example, your choice of research methods – should make little difference to your project design in terms of your choice and usage of your scholarly theory and methodology. Here your business theory and methodology should drive all parts of your project structure as the motivation for your project arises: a) from one or more gaps that you have identified in your business literature; and b) from your methodology which you (should) believe will best form your basis for addressing those gaps and guide your choice of tools (research methods) that will help you address your RQ.

Research question

In the same way as your RQ has formed the basis of your current project, your RQ can constitute the most important learning outcome from your project. In Chapter 1 we explained the importance of developing a motivating and researchable RQ for your project. What can you take away from your RQ long after you will have forgotten what that RQ was?

Remembering your project RQ is not your critical takeaway from your project after you have completed it – as an RQ that will motivate you personally in your research is normally developed for each project (although as an academic or professional researcher with a research workplan, you may be seeking to address different aspects of an RQ across discrete projects). However, what you must make a point of remembering is the process in which you formed your RQ, as it is the *discipline* of developing a single, powerful RQ that will be useful in your academic or professional career. Why?

Recall that your RQ was able to capture the critical gap that formed the rationale for your research *and* it also motivated you personally to undertake your research. The importance of remembering the discipline of this process is that in undertaking future projects you will be able to balance *your own interests* in undertaking any project by embedding those interests within the streams of knowledge in and about your topic of research. The way that you may continue to use this process therefore holds your key to creating lasting impact in future projects.

Hopefully, your current business project has prompted you to discover and recognize – with humility – that knowledge does exist on your topic and that other researchers have explored your topic before you. (Remember here our warning not to fall into the trap of many business projects when students suggest there is little (or worse, no) literature on their topic – when what they mean is that little has been written about their subject or theme – which of course is hardly surprising when your interests are personal to you.)

Literature exists somewhere on every business and management topic, and researchers' typical problem is to be able to synthesize a vast body of literature on a topic, and not whether there may be enough literature on it.

By contrast, in your choice of literature and theory it can be extremely difficult to convince examiners that theory does not exist to explain your phenomenon when in fact theory exists and it is you who have failed to discover it! We have suggested that a general rule is to avoid a topic if you believe that, for whatever reason, you cannot locate enough literature on that topic. However, you should also have discovered that you have been able to continue researching your subject organization even where you have changed the literature behind your subject.

In learning why this is so, let us turn again to your dream holiday. Suppose that your subject is your destination, and that your topic is a certain attraction for you at your destination. Midway through your planning you discover that you cannot locate much literature on your chosen topic – namely, your star attraction. Will you be fazed by this and change your destination? We bet you won't! Instead, will you not visit the same destination and locate other literature on other attractions and visit those? Adapting your interests in this way – contingency planning – is part of the normal practice of all academic research, in big and small projects.

In small student projects, apart from changing the literature behind your research, you may also find that you do not have enough good data on your case or target firm. If so you will need to be imaginative in locating enough data through alternative means, such as from speaking to former employees and customers (your student friends!) of your case firm if you cannot access current employees or cannot secure enough good data from them. Here a Plan B and even Plan C (if your access to data is difficult) would be very sensible as you know you must obtain enough good data, both primary and secondary, in order for you to gain at least a pass in your project.

Let us summarize your process of developing a motivating and researchable RQ as an aide-memoire for your future career:

- Motivation: What really intrigues me about my organization, and why? What is known and not known about the problem I have identified?

- Research-ability: What (scholarly) theory am I familiar with and I can draw on to explore and explain this problem? Equally, is my methodology suitable for me to carry out my research?

(Adapted from Watson, 1994)

Remember: If you cannot articulate your research problem in a short, punchy RQ that addresses the above criteria, then you have not satisfactorily planned your research – your dream holiday. If so, please rethink the above exercise! Would you accept going on your holiday unless you have fixed your costs and other structural aspects of your trip?

Knowledge of cutting-edge research and theory

In Chapter 1 we set out the nature of literature and theory and then in Chapter 6 we guided you in applying your knowledge to interpret and draw conclusions from your findings to answer your RQ. What have you learned from studying and using literature in this way? Here we want to suggest two learning outcomes from your experience of literature that may fall beyond your current project. First, from your current exercise you will have developed practical knowledge of a wide range of sources for locating literature not only in, but also about and around, your subject. This literature may not directly concern your subject, but you will have learned to identify and locate your subject within a business field.

Equally importantly, you will have learned a range of sources for locating pertinent literature beyond merely relying on Google Scholar!

These sources should have included high-quality search engines that your university subscribes to for accessing scholarly journal articles (Web of Science, Business Source Premier, EBSCO etc) and should also have drawn from your own practical system for tracing and recording references from key publications in your literature. All this requires close knowledge of what the key publications are in this literature and an organized way of recording your references, for example through Endnote, so that you may build a comprehensive list of the key works in your literature. (Endnote is a downloadable software program that offers a convenient way to automatically format and manage bibliographies with patented bibliography technology. Please check if your university is licensed to use the software, which will allow you free access: www.myendnoteweb.com/EndNoteWeb.html.) Knowledge of your various sources of literature and referencing constitute important elements of your experience in any type of research you may undertake in future.

A second useful takeaway from your knowledge and application of theory is your understanding of the nature of theory and how good theory may be used to explain and predict possible outcomes from your research *before* you embark on this journey.

As professional researchers, we believe that an understanding of *how* you may use theory is one of the most important lessons that we have to teach you. Too many managers believe that theory is 'too complicated'. Now, if you too believe that you are not a theory-driven person and are more inclined to think practically and not theoretically, think again. Theory is intensely practical, and without acknowledging it you will probably have used theory for much of your professional life. For example, whenever you have planned for any activity – including your dream holiday – your plans would have been based on your own theory that your actions would produce a certain, imagined outcome. You should not therefore believe that using theory in the normal course of your professional life is somehow unsuitable for you – 'not my thing' is the refrain we have heard from many of our project students. This is a mistaken view, which if you persist in holding makes no sense: a) because you already practise theory personally and professionally; and b) because you are denying an important lesson in what you have paid for in your business school education.

In sum, this lesson is to clarify and build on a process of theorizing – honing your skills in using theory in a highly practical way – that you have already been practising in the business world. In studying theory you will have understood the logic of this last statement as business and management theory is developed from observation of real-world phenomena.

Research tools

The final element we have listed that can impact significantly on your future career is the learning you have derived from selecting and using research methods as practical tools.

We have already suggested the importance of your learning about methodology in framing your research. In Parts 2 and 3 of this book we have also set out in detail how you may collect and analyse data by selecting and using suitable methods. Again, there are at least two important lessons from this learning that can impact significantly on your future career.

First, you should not forget the methods we have described and the way that they should be used in producing important findings that will contribute significantly to your chosen literature. You will encounter most if not all the methods we have described either as a manager or a business academic as they are useful methods for conducting any research project, which explains the continuing popularity of surveys, interviews etc.

Second, just as with other elements in structuring your project, the *process* in which you conducted your research – as well as an awareness of alternative processes in which your research may have been conducted – constitutes important lessons that can impact significantly on your career. In future you may need to practise and refresh your skill in developing good survey questions or in applying statistical tools to analyse data; but like riding a bicycle you will not forget how research is conducted as the skills involved in doing so are a core and normal part of business administration. It follows from this that even if you do not personally conduct another piece of research for the rest of your life, as a manager you should be familiar with the ways in which data are collected, analysed and reported about organizations, including your own. As knowledge of the research process involves foundational skills of business administration, it also follows that your career advancement in business organizations will depend at least partly on your ability to build on the skills that you have learned in collecting, analysing and reporting data in order to gain deeper knowledge of your own organization and of competitor organizations.

Having read and reflected on our advice you are now ready to take away your learning and make a lasting impact on your career!

Just as with your dream holiday, the more carefully you have planned for your research the more enjoyable it is likely to be. The best thing about a dream holiday is that your greatest enjoyment from it – its biggest impact – will emerge in years to come when you recall your experience of your holiday... and then seek to recreate that experience by going on another dream holiday to a different destination. This would be the equivalent of using your experience of past projects to design a new project and address the criteria in this chapter for setting it up. Using your learning in this way would maximize your impact from a truly memorable experience!

Reference

Watson, T (1994) Managing, crafting and researching: words, skill, and imagination in shaping management research, *British Journal of Management*, 5(Supplement S1), S77–S87

INDEX

(*italics* indicate a figure or table in the text)

CPSIA information can be obtained at www.ICGtesting.com
Printed in the USA
BVOW01s1004231014

372050BV00008B/280/P

A big advantage of the repertory grid technique is that it allows interviewees to articulate their experience in the way they see the world, according to their own personal constructs. It avoids interviewer bias and because it uses differences and similarities with other examples, it can be easier to tease out the interviewee's views.

The repertory grid technique, therefore, can be a rich source of qualitative data and allow people to express things in their own terms or jargon. Because it also uses rating scales, it can also be analysed statistically, hence it combines both qualitative and quantitative methodology.

Kelly developed the repertory grid technique based on his theory to enable structured conversations between researcher and participant and explorations of the individual's world of meaning. Unlike standard approaches to research, such as questionnaires and interviews, the repertory grid can elicit people's constructs without influencing them by the researcher's preconceived questions.

The main components of a repertory grid:

1. The topic – what the interview is about.

2. Elements – these are examples that illustrate the topic. They can be people, objects, experiences, events, according to the topic. The elements can either be chosen by the interviewee, or they can be preselected.

3. Constructs – the most important component of the repertory grid. This is where the elements are compared with one another to produce a series of statements which describe what the interviewee thinks about the topic. These statements will form the eventual unit of analysis. They will be bipolar – in other words, every statement will be presented as opposite ends of a pole.

4. Ratings – once the main constructs and elements are in place, they are entered on a grid with the elements on top and the constructs down the side. The interviewee then rates each element against each construct according to a rating scale, usually of 1–5.

Uses of a repertory grid

Because of its ability to capture good data, the repertory grid is used in a wide range of contexts. For example:

- human resources (eg performance appraisals, job analysis, training needs analysis, staff and organizational development);
- psychology (for example, psychological tests or counselling-type interviews);
- brand analysis and consumer behaviour;
- team development and organizational studies; and
- information retrieval studies and systems analysis.

For example, suppose a student is asked about their experience of lectures. The interviewer might ask, 'What makes a good lecturer?' If the student struggled to respond, the interviewer might give a couple of prompts, perhaps based on his or her conception of what qualities a good lecturer should possess. With the repertory grid technique, the student and the interviewer could agree on a range of particular lecturers and then use a technique of comparison and contrast as a way of getting the student to talk.

It is particularly good in circumstances where it is important to understand how people think, for teasing out knowledge that is implicit rather than explicit, and for establishing mental maps.

Advantages and drawbacks of a repertory grid

- It is time-consuming; each interview will take up to an hour.
- It can appear rather artificial, and senior managers in particular may be sceptical about its value, and hence rather unwilling to give time to it.
- There are many variations of design and it can be difficult to select the right one.
- The analysis process can 'overwhelm with numbers' and one can become fascinated by the process of computer analysis and what it can 'discover' – at the expense of the 'bigger picture'.

References

Adolphis, M, How to... use mixed methods research, p 1: www.emeraldinsight.com/research/guides/methods/mixed_methods.htm?PHPSESSID=pmn9sfct8ieo1u4u0lga7ff9u5)

Beech, BF (1997) Studying the future: a Delphi survey of how multi-disciplinary clinical staff view the likely development of two community mental health centres over the course of the next two years, *Journal of Advanced Nursing*, 25, 331–38

Briedenhann, J and Butts, S (2006) Application of the Delphi Technique to Rural Tourism Project Evaluation, *Current Issues in Tourism*, 9(2), 171–90

Cargan, L (2007) *Doing Social Research*, Rowman and Littlefield Inc, Maryland, US

Chan, APC, Yung, EHK, Lam, PTI, Tam, CM and Cheung, SO (2001) Application of Delphi Method in selection of procurement systems for construction projects, *Construction Management and Economics*, 19, 699–718

Coakes E, and Smith PA, (2007) Communities of Practice and Change-Supporting Innovation, *Journal of Knowledge Management Practice – The Knowledge Garden*, Vol 8, Special Issue 1, May 2007, www.tlainc.com/jkmpv8si107.htm

Corotis, RFR and Harris, J (1981) Delphi Method: theory and design load applications, *Journal of the Structural Division ASCE*, 107 (6), 1095–105

Creswell, JW and Clark, VLP (2007) *Designing and Conducting Mixed Methods Research*, Sage, Thousand Oaks, CA

Dalkey, N and O Helmer, O (1963) An Experimental Application of the Delphi Method to a Group of Experts, *Management Science*, 9 (3), 458–67

Daniel, EM and White, A (2005) The Future of Inter-Organisational System Linkages: Findings of an International Delphi Study, *European Journal of Information Systems*, 14, 188–203

DeWalt, KM, DeWalt, BR (2011) *Participant Observation: A Guide for Fieldworkers*, 2nd edition, Altimira Press, Plymouth

Goodchild, MF (2007) Citizens as sensors: the world of volunteered geography, *GeoJournal* , 69, 211–21

Gordon, TJ (1994) The Delphi method, *Futures research methodology*, 1–33

Grafton, J, Lillis, AM, Mahama, H (2011) Mixed methods research in accounting, *Qualitative Research in Accounting & Management*, 8 (1), 5–21

Helmer, O (1977) Problems in futures research: delphi and causal cross-impact analysis, *Futures*, February, 17–31

Holsapple, CW and Joshi, KD (2000) An investigation of factors that influence the management of knowledge in organisations, *The Journal of Strategic Information Systems*, 9(2), 235–61

Howe, J (2008) *Why the Power of the Crowd Is Driving the Future of Business*, Crown Business, New York, NY

Jankowicz, D and Dick, P (2001) A social constructionist account of police culture and its influence on the representation and progression of female officers: A repertory grid analysis in a UK police force, published in Policing, *An International Journal of Police Strategies & Management*, 24(2), 181–99

JISC (2010) Joint Information Systems Committee, Capturing the Power of the Crowd and the Challenge of Community Collections, available at: www.jisc.ac.uk/publications/jiscinform/2010/~/link.aspx?_id=0ED8E52 991054128B38E24FA31C8E9A4&_z=z, accessed January 24th 2012

Johnson, RB and Anthony, J Onwuegbuzie (2004) Mixed methods research: a research paradigm whose time has come, *Educational Researcher*, October 2004, 33(7), 14–26

Kelly, G (1955) *The Psychology of Personal Constructs: Volumes One and Two*, Routledge, London

Knoke, D and Yang, S (2008) *Social Network Analysis*, Second Edition, Sage, London

Linstone, HA (1978) *The Delphi Technique* Westport, Connecticut, Greenwood

Loughlin K and Moore L (1979) Using Delphi to achieve congruent objectives and activities in a pediatrics department, *Journal of Medical Education*, 54, 101–106

MacCarthy, BL and Atthirawong, W (2003) Factors affecting location decisions in international operations – a Delphi Study, *International Journal of Operations & Production Management*, 23(7), 33–45

McKenna, HP (1994) The Delphi technique: a worthwhile research approach for nursing, *Journal of Advanced Nursing*, 19(6), 1221–25

McKnight, J (1991) The Delphi Approach to Strategic Planning, *Nursing Management*, 22 (4), 55–57

Okoli, C and Pawlowski, SD (2004) The Delphi method as a research tool: an example, design consideration and applications, *Information and Management*, 42(1), 15–29

Reason, PE (1994) *Participation in Human Inquiry*, Sage Publications, London

Reid, N (1988) *The Delphi Technique: Its Contribution to the Evaluation of Professional Practice*, Chapman & Hall, New York

Sun, PYT and Scott, JT (2005) An investigation of barriers to knowledge transfer, *Journal of Knowledge Management*, 9(2), 75–90